The Girl Who Climbed Everest

Bonita Norris

The Girl Who Climbed Everest

HODDER

First published in Great Britain in 2017 by Hodder & Stoughton
An Hachette UK company

A CIP catalogue record for this title is
available from the British Library

Hardback ISBN 978 1 473 64975 0
Trade paperback ISBN 978 1 473 64977 4
Ebook ISBN 978 1 473 64976 7

Typeset in Sabon MT by Palimpsest Book Production Ltd,
Falkirk, Stirlingshire

Printed and bound by Clays Ltd, St Ives plc

Hodder & Stoughton policy is to use papers that are natural, renewable
and recyclable products and made from wood grown in sustainable forests.
The logging and manufacturing processes are expected to conform
to the environmental regulations of the country of origin.

Hodder & Stoughton Ltd
Carmelite House
50 Victoria Embankment
London EC4Y 0DZ

www.hodder.co.uk

For
My love, Adrian
&
My Parents

My heart pounds in my chest: 180 beats per minute. Just feeling it straining against my ribcage makes me panic. I try to suck air into my lungs. My entire body heaves with the rise and fall of my chest, helping my lungs to take in as much oxygen as possible. I grimace. My body has been working this hard all day. It's exhausted and sore just from trying to breathe.

I'm not even moving. I'm lying on my sleeping mat in our tent at the highest camp on Mount Everest, at 8,000 metres above sea level. To my left is my teammate Tom, and on my right is Rick and our leader Kenton. We are top to tail and elbow to elbow. Nobody talks. It's taken nearly two years of training and hard graft to get this far. If all goes to plan, we are just fifteen hours away from achieving our dreams – to reach the highest point on planet Earth.

Our tent is perched on the South Col on Everest's South East Ridge, 880 metres below the summit. Beyond the fabric of our orange cocoon, a mere millimetre away, is an unfamiliar world – both beautiful and brutal. An ocean of cloud simmers below us. Through the frothy white expanse, distant peaks soar upwards like floating islands. The early evening light bathes the jagged spires in a fiery orange glow. These Himalayan giants are some of the highest in the world – and yet here we are, sitting in our tent looking down on them. It's glorious.

Up here above the weather, we are truly on the cusp of another world. It feels as if we're on another planet. But as the hours pass, the insidious grip of hypoxia and deadly cold starts to tighten around us. We are not in space, we are somewhere else – below the stars, in the heavens of Earth. In this realm of the gods, nature and good fortune rule. It's a place that humans have not and will not ever conquer. To even enter this world, we must be willing to offer our lives as a sacrifice. We are at its mercy.

Arriving at Camp Four a few hours earlier, I had staggered over the shale and loose rock, feeling as though I'd reached the end of the world. Camp Four is our highest and final camp, pitched on a desolate patch of earth. I could see our orange tent ahead – up here, its colour seemed dulled and the wind battering the fabric became the only sound I could distinguish. My reactions were so slow. All my senses seemed to be shutting down. To get to this point had taken a gargantuan effort. A month of climbing up towards the 'death zone', above 8,000 metres. With every step there was less oxygen, less warmth, and less chance that we would ever return home.

Now, collapsed in the tent, I'm gasping for air. I tear off my oxygen mask. It makes no sense to rip it off, but it feels so claustrophobic: every time I breathe in, the mask gets sucked on to my face and I feel as if I'm being suffocated. The effect of being able to breathe cold air deep into my lungs, even if it is almost devoid of oxygen, instantly calms me down.

We settle in: rolling out our sleeping mats, pulling out

our sleeping bags and chucking our backpacks into the rear of the tent. We're all crammed in together with our oxygen tanks and tubes. Then comes the task of taking off our boots. Frozen fingers tackle frozen laces. The effort to pull off my heavy plastic outer boot requires a deep breath and then an all-out struggle.

Finally, after freeing my feet of the layers of socks and boots and outer boots, I'm ready to creep into my sleeping bag for a precious few minutes' sleep. I'm so tired my bones ache. I've not slept properly in days. Only adrenaline is keeping me awake.

All I can think about is timings – the clock is ticking, four hours to go until we set off. I've got twenty minutes to try and get some rest before I have to start going through my checklists and getting ready for our one and only shot at the summit.

Lying here, I can feel the mountain digging into me. My wasted body is nearly two stone lighter than when I set off from Gatwick Airport only six weeks ago. My spine and pelvis jut out and dig into the ice and rock; there is no layer of fat to offer any protection. I try and shuffle about but there's not enough room. Tom is already snoring next to me; Rick is lying there not making a sound. We are buried under a mountain of down sleeping bags, the vapour from our breath condensing in the air and making everything damp and sticky.

Lying still allows my mind to start to wander. For a few moments at least, I'm not distracted by clipping karabiners, rope work or regulating my oxygen bottle. Without those distractions, the things eating away at me start to surface again. It's these quiet moments that are always the hardest

– when you really start to fight with your own thoughts.

I start to think about my family. Home, way down the Western Cwm, across the Khumbu Valley and over the horizon, thousands of miles across the planet, and five vertical miles below me.

Home is a pretty lemon-posset-coloured house in Wokingham in Berkshire, surrounded by half an acre of garden and tall oak trees. I have lived there from the age of thirteen. Growing up, I'd set myself time trials in the garden – like trying to see how quickly I could run from the back fence, past the apple tree, around the pond, past the house to the front, dodge my mum's car, skid down the grass and jump the brambles, maybe even try a forward roll as I landed, and sprint past the rose bushes up to the end of the front garden, trying to better my record each time.

Home is also my family: my mum, stepdad, two brothers and two cats, Bubbles and Tinkerbell. I remember packing for my first ever Himalayan expedition to Mount Manaslu, the world's eighth highest peak, when I was 20 years old. The cats (kittens then) wouldn't leave my 150-litre kitbag alone, and I kept finding them curled up asleep in it.

Bubbles would sometimes sleep in my bed at night so, for Everest, my mum has bought me a hot-water bottle with a furry leopard-print cover, so that at night I can cuddle that instead. Some of my happiest moments on the mountain are sleeping at Base Camp and hearing the glacier crack beneath me, knowing I'm in this magical place but with my furry hot-water bottle reminding me of Bubbles, keeping me connected to home.

I don't have my hot-water bottle now. It was too heavy

to carry. Up here, I am going to use my hard plastic drinking bottle instead. I'll fill the bottle with hot water and put it into a sock and cuddle that – though it's definitely not the same as cuddling Bubbles.

I think about how isolated we are, how cold and desolate it is outside. I start to yearn for home. I miss warmth. I miss summer. As a teenager I would drag my duvet into the garden and lie there all day in the sun, reading books and looking up at the passing clouds. Right now, I would give *anything* to be lying in the sun in my garden, instead of the cold hard ice in the death zone on Everest. I wonder if I'll ever get to lie on the grass on a summer's day again. Going to the extremes and getting so close to the line between life and death changes your perspective. You suddenly crave the simplest of things – the feel of breeze on your skin, the fresh air, the sky. You feel lucky to be alive.

The more I think about home, the more I miss it. I haven't heard my mum's voice in six weeks. I miss her so much. What if I never see her again? The next twenty-four hours are going to be the most dangerous of my life. Should I try to ring her on Tom's sat phone to say goodbye?

I've felt this pit in my stomach before. That desperate homesickness that physically hurts, when you would give everything you had just to wake up in your own bed or give your little brother a hug. It was on my first Himalayan expedition in 2009 that I was first homesick. I was 21 years old and had never before been so scared or out of my comfort zone.

Manaslu is a striking mountain flanked by huge glaciers and avalanche-prone slopes, and is located in one of the most remote parts of Nepal. If something went wrong, there was little chance of rescue; I was truly being thrown in at the deep end.

Every day on Manaslu would seem like the hardest day of my life – but then the next day would be even harder. I was by far the most inexperienced on our team. I was constantly intimidated and felt as if I was making every mistake in the book. I thought I was a pretty good climber, but Manaslu showed me I wasn't. I could never have imagined the depths of physical and mental endurance I would have to go through; could never have foreseen some of the scary situations in which I'd have to hold my nerve.

Every day, I wanted to give up. Every day, I wanted to be at home. There were times when I would shut my eyes and pray that I was back at home. I would open them again to find towers of ice soaring above me, the wind blasting my cheeks red raw, knowing there were still many more hours of climbing before the solace of a tent and sleeping bag. I was a million miles away from home. That realisation was almost too much to bear.

I have never been so terrified or so broken. All the time, I cursed myself for being so stupid as to sign up in the first place. I told myself I wasn't cut out for being a mountaineer. I swore I'd never go near another mountain. And yet here I am again, this time on Everest, feeling the exact same way. Why did I come back? Why didn't I learn my lesson?

The reason I'm here on Everest is because of just *one* moment on Manaslu. After pushing through the hardest day of climbing, we finally escaped from the shadows and found ourselves high above the clouds. Up here on the open summit fields, I finally felt I could relax. With the sun shining and the deep blue sky interrupted only by miles of white Himalayan peaks as far as the eye could see, I found myself climbing alone, my teammates all ahead of me. I felt as though I had the whole of the Himalayas to myself.

I hurried on, not wanting to get left too far behind. My feet crunched on the hard snow, my breathing immediately strained from the lack of oxygen. I tried to focus and find a rhythm. Suddenly, a gust of wind whipped around me and blew a layer of ice crystals high into the air. I found myself surrounded by billions of tiny shards of ice dancing in the sunlight. As they gently fell back to earth, they glittered like fairy dust. I swear I could hear them tingling with energy.

Walking through those ice crystals was like being bathed in magic. A smile broke out across my cheeks. A feeling of pure joy rose in my chest. My spirit soared. I was *so glad* I hadn't given up when I most wanted to. I was so glad I had the courage to leave the comforts of home and fight my way up this mountain because, if I hadn't, I would never have seen something as rare and beautiful as this. I would never have felt those delicate crystals melt upon my cheeks, and felt as though somehow the mountain was trying to tell me everything was going to be OK.

In that moment, I think I came alive. I left behind my anxious teenage self and became a woman and a mountaineer. I realised that I was far more capable than I first thought, and that, just when I'd wanted to give up, I'd had so much more to give. I saw the amazing things that happen when we step outside our comfort zones.

We subsequently reached the false summit of Mount Manaslu, and I became one of the youngest people ever to climb to it. I pushed on and I've never been so grateful that I did. That moment on Manaslu is why I'm here, now, in the death zone on Mount Everest, just hours away from leaving our tent and heading out into the darkness to the top of the world.

This is a book about those moments – the smallest moments that define your path for ever. It's about the pain and distress of leaving your comfort zone – and the extraordinary things that happen when you do. It's about everything I learnt on the side of a mountain: how to overcome fear, how to push on when you least want to, and how there is so much more out there than you think. I truly believe that all it takes to make your dreams come true is hard work and self-belief. Trust me: if I can do it, anyone can.

I open my eyes and peer over my sleeping bag. Wind is battering the tent walls as though it's trying to attack us – punching and kicking at the fabric, antagonising us, daring us to step outside again.

Kenton, our leader, is hunched over a little stove with a battered pan on top, heating up a lump of ice to make water. It's time to start 'boiling', as we call it – the process of melting ice for water, which for four people will take many hours. We need to rehydrate, by mixing the water with powdered soups, tea or fruit flavouring, then we need to boil enough water for each climber to take at least a litre with them on the summit climb. Fifteen hours out on the mountain with only a litre of water. And you know what? Most people get back to camp after their summit ordeal having only had a few sips.

'Soup?' Kenton hands me a plastic bottle filled with some boiled water and a minestrone powder. I gulp the salty fluids and then I see Kenton's face contort with horror.

'What?'

'I've just realised that's my pee bottle. Sorry!'

Honestly, I find it funny. It's just the kind of thing Kenton would do.

After that gulp of soup, I force myself to eat something. Eating is increidbly difficult in the death zone – it feels like another mountain to climb. But I have to do it because I know the energy will keep me alive. I manage some salami and two Dairylea triangles. I can't stomach anything else. Neither can my teammates.

The countdown is on. We have three hours to get ready before we leave the tent at 9 p.m. Our plan is to climb through the night to reach the summit of Mount Everest for sunrise.

Once you're in the death zone, there's no such thing as rest. Every second we spend up here, above 8,000 metres, our bodies are starved of oxygen. The fact that I can't eat even a little food is the first sign – my stomach has shut down. My body sees it as a non-vital organ in comparison to my brain and my heart, so it's the first thing to stop functioning. We are slowly dying and it's terrifying. We're on a race against time. Sleeping is not an option – we have to get to the summit as fast as we can, and then get the hell out of here.

Three hours might seem a long time just to get dressed for the summit, but everything takes so much longer when our brains are fuzzy, reaction times dulled, and our bodies so tired. I have to dress myself in thermal leggings and an Icebreaker top, then a fleece and finally – over the top – my down suit. It's a £900 onesie, the most expensive outfit I've ever owned. It's stuffed with the feathers of Siberian geese, which live in some of the coldest conditions in the world, so their down is supremely good at trapping body heat – it will keep me alive in temperatures as low as minus 40°C.

Luckily, tonight it's around minus 25°C, with no wind. It's not so much the air temperature that gets you – it's the wind chill. A 20 km/h wind can make the temperature feel as low as minus 43°C. In 2004 wind speeds of 280 km/h were recorded near the summit. I pray that our weather forecasts are correct and that we won't be surprised with gusts strong enough to blow us clean off the mountain.

I'm only wearing three layers in total. It sounds risky to wear so little, but the down suit will only warm up prop-erly if my body heat is reaching it and getting trapped in the down. There have been horror stories in the past where inexperienced climbers have nearly frozen to death because they were wearing a waterproof jacket – or 'hard shell' as we call it – under their down suit. They thought the extra layer would keep them warmer, but it did the exact oppo-site: it stopped body heat reaching the down fibres in the suit, so the suit wasn't warming up and creating the hot microclimate that keeps us alive.

I have many hacks that were learned over time and by making mistakes – I put my hand-warmer sachets into my oxygen mask, so that the chemicals react with the oxygen and start to heat up. Up here in the death zone, even hand warmers don't work properly in the oxygen-starved atmosphere. I put spare batteries into my sports bra – next to my heart. Here, they'll be kept warm from my body heat and I'll have them ready for emergencies.

Tick, tick, tick – down the checklist I go. I have goals I need to achieve by certain times – boiling my water at the right time, going to the loo, and changing my oxygen bottle over to a fresh canister. The minutes and hours are slipping away from me. I try not to think about the fact that every time a task is completed, the closer I am to leaving the tent.

I feel strong and weak at the same time. I feel as if I'm moving in slow motion. Everything takes a huge effort. I have to lie down and take a break after pulling each sock on. My tolerance to pain and suffering is reaching its limit and the smallest things are starting to get to me. As I start to pull on my thermal leggings, I realise that my skin is dry and flaking. Most of my body hasn't seen daylight or a proper wash for many weeks now.

I run through my checklists. Have I got everything? Have I got spares? Can I get to everything I need quickly in an emergency? My brain is fuzzy. I can't remember things I just did, or do simple sums. I check my oxygen regulator to work out how long the bottle will last, but the calculation is almost too much for me. Two litres per minute in a 720-litre pressurised bottle will last ... six hours?

I take a second to calm my heart rate and then I start to finally put on my boots. This requires a monumental effort. I have an inner boot and an outer boot and each takes five minutes to do up properly, because I need to rest every few seconds from the exertion. They have laces and zips and they have to be done up perfectly – too tight and the blood won't be able to circulate properly; too loose and I'll get blisters and won't be able to walk. My fingers don't seem to be responding to my brain. They're cold too, and as I pull the laces, the friction tears into my frozen skin. The sharp pain raises my heart rate even higher.

Suddenly, it's 8.45 p.m. and I'm starting to feel scared. Many better mountaineers than me have died on Everest summit night. This mountain is steeped in history and ghosts. I wonder if I'll end up like them. I think about the movies and books written about disasters on Everest – what if people are going to be writing about tonight one day?

I think about Rob Hall, who died below the Hillary Step because he was simply unable to muster the energy to move any longer, unable to climb up and over the South Summit. He died because he didn't have the energy to get up – that could happen to me. I could freeze to death on the mountain.

I'm scared of getting altitude sickness and my lungs filling with fluid till I drown. I'm scared I'll get so cold that I'll get frostbite. There's so much I can't control. Rock fall. Bad weather. I get visions of falling into space, rope slipping from my fingers.

I'm afraid of the pain. The pain of lifting each foot off the ground is almost too much. I can't bear the thought of putting my body through so much suffering again. At this point, it feels utterly impossible. We're looking at a fifteen-hour round trip – it seems incomprehensible right now. Surely we can't survive for that long out there?

The tent is so comforting – the warm orange glow, the walls shutting off the reality of the outside world. I start to imagine the world beyond the tent. It's one of the most extreme environments on the planet. Totally unforgiving. I think about the dark and cold slowly tightening its grip around us. All I have to protect me is my down suit and a mask. Better to stay here. The pull of the tent is so strong, it's almost physical. My instincts start screaming at me to stay where it's safe.

I feel panic rising in my chest. Trussed up in my heavy down suit, goggles, oxygen mask and boots, I am trapped. Beads of sweat start percolating on my forehead. I feel cumbersome and get the urge to rip everything off. My skeletal body under all this weight feels almost too weak to stand. I don't want to be here. I want to be anywhere but here.

It's 8.55 p.m. My teammates are making final checks, and then, like awkward astronauts in their stiff space suits and masks, Tom, Rick and Kenton roll out of the tent one by one and disappear into the darkness. They are expecting me to be right behind them, but now, alone in the tent, I am terrified of what lies beyond. If I step outside, will I ever make it back? I feel paralysed with fear; my body refuses to move.

I know this feeling. I've been completely overwhelmed by it many times in the past. I don't want to go, but I know that if I can just step out of the tent, everything will fall into place. I'll do what I've trained myself to do.

'This is it,' I tell myself. 'This is what you've been working towards for nearly two years, two years of dreaming and hoping – so bloody get on with it!' But I can't make myself leave the tent.

I search for a way to convince myself to move. My team-mates are getting impatient. I can hear them outside – their strained voices muffled by the plastic masks over their faces. I say to myself, 'Don't think about anything else. All you have to do is step outside the tent. If you don't like it, you can come back inside. Just one step – that's it. No big deal. You can do it.'

All I have to do is one little step, then I can give up. Just one step, and then it's all over if I want it to be. I focus on the doorway and the inky black beyond. 'One step is all you have to do. Take a leap of faith.'

With that, I drag myself to the door, and stand up outside. I feel unsteady on my feet. An instant flush of bitter cold settles into my bones. The night is deadly silent. I turn to Kenton. His head torch blinds me, but I can hear him behind his mask. 'Let's go,' he says. And just like that, we begin to move.

The hardest part is behind me. Now all I have to do is climb.

CHAPTER 2

'This is when you decide whether you want to be a runner, or a very good runner.'

People are shocked when they find out that less than two years before I stood on the summit of Mount Everest, I had never climbed a mountain. Not a single snow-covered peak.

I was born in 1987 and I grew up in Wokingham in Berkshire, where there are no mountains at all. In fact, I think the highest point in Wokingham is 74 metres above sea level.

I could easily overly romanticise my upbringing, but I'm going to try not to, because all in all it was very ordinary. My younger brother Harry and I were very loved, very supported and very lucky. We were very privileged, not in the sense of wealth, but privileged because we had great parents who would do anything for us. We went to the local comprehensives and got to go on holidays to France, Turkey or Spain in the summer. As far as I was concerned, it was the best upbringing in the world. I knew we were lucky, and I wouldn't have changed a thing.

I was five years old when my parents divorced and Harry was three. They married at nineteen and had me when my dad, Patrick was twenty-eight and my mum, Jacqui was twenty-four.

My mum was one of four and the daughter of an ice-cream man. Grandad had a plastic cow stuck to the top of his van and would embarrass her greatly whenever he picked her up from seeing her friends. My mum was a model and worked hard from the age of twelve, going to London for castings alone and fitting in her jobs around school work – or not, as it turned out. She earned all her own money and was fiercely independent.

Dad was the fourth of six children and had spent his toddler years in Aden in Yemen whilst my grandad was posted there, before the family moved to Bracknell when my dad was eight years old. He left home at fourteen and began working as a builder, and by the time he was eighteen he was running his own building firm.

He and my mum met in a pub in Bracknell, and they were married at Bracknell Parish Church not long after. They were married for twelve years before going their separate ways. Throughout their separation, mum and dad always made my brother and I see the positives – two Christmases and birthdays, two bedrooms, two sets of summer holidays. It was a way to distract us and it worked. I never felt caught in the middle or made to choose between them. They really were brilliant and did the best for us kids. I have never been affected by my parents' divorce as a result. We were and still are incredibly blessed to stay a tight-knit family.

After my parents separated, my mum met Rob. Rob was only twenty-seven when he agreed to take on the role of step-father to two raving mad kids. His friends told him over a pint in their local pub to run for the hills – what was he doing thinking of having a serious relationship with a woman who had two children? He said, 'I don't care, I'll do anything to be with her and I'll work it out.' From mine and Harry's perspective, Rob was lucky to have a ready-made family – we thought he'd hit the jackpot. Harry and I thought he would also find it funny when we put tuna or Play-Doh into his milk carton, purposely broke his football trophies, jammed a spoon into his brand-new video player, jumped into his baths whenever he ran one and generally ruined any semblance of his twenty-seven-year-old once single self. His transition into fatherhood was a baptism of fire to say the least.

For me, growing up in Wokingham's great outdoors meant sitting on the swings in the local park, playing street hockey with the neighbours, or cycling around our estate, Keep Hatch Farm, at breakneck speed to buy sweets from the corner shop and, once, while chasing a friend on his bike, riding straight into a lamppost and breaking my arm. I was a self-proclaimed 'Sporty Spice', even with a plaster cast up to my armpit.

At weekends we went to my dad's in Bracknell, where he'd built us a tree house with a fireman's pole. I loved it, and whether it was summer or winter Harry and I would be out in the garden making up games, catching snails and jumping out of the tree house. I would boss Harry around as much as he would let me. Mostly though he just wanted to set fire to things. We had a dog called Candy and we would go on big walks, followed by a weekly bonfire in the garden, which was Harry's favourite. At the time, my dad was getting himself back on his feet after the financial crash hit the construction industry hard in the early 1990s. He never let anything get in the way of having fun with his kids and was always a hands-on dad – from pizza nights where he would make dough and then my brother and I would pile on mountains of toppings, to creating elaborate Easter egg hunts with hand-drawn maps and riddles that would take us what felt like hours to solve.

Holidays with him then were wonderfully simple: weekends on the coast or wild camping in the New Forest, where my brother and I would never listen to my dad and would both go running after the ponies, to try and stroke them. Deservedly, we both got badly kicked. I remember my mother's horror when we got home from one trip and I had a horseshoe-shaped black bruise on my leg.

By the time I was ten, I remember climbing up a tree with a boy I fancied from my school. We sat awkwardly on one of the branches about 8 metres off the ground, barely talking and definitely not sharing our first kiss. That tree overlooked a building site, and a few times that summer Harry and I would go roaming over the piles of rubble and across timbers into the half-finished houses, sitting with our legs hanging out of the window frames of huge master bedrooms. There were woods nearby, where we would build dens and be convinced that homeless people lived in the bushes and were trying to 'get us'.

We were always outdoors, until one of the kids on the estate, David, got a Sky Box and had channels like Cartoon Network. He wouldn't come out and play any more, and after that things changed. The boys, including Harry, got given PlayStations for Christmas instead of roller blades or a new bike. I turned eleven years old in October 1998 and had a Spice Girls party and wore make-up for the first time. We were starting to grow up.

Shortly after my birthday I started going to an athletics club twice a week at Bracknell Athletics. On Tuesday night we would meet at the track and then go for a run around the estates nearby, one of the volunteers at the front, about twenty of us kids in the middle, and another volunteer at the back.

It was my dad who had first taken me to athletics, after I had decided I didn't like horse riding or karate or ballet any more. I remember that first training session – we ran straight out of the stadium and off into the streets. I remember the tightness in my chest because of everyone running in pairs, and me not knowing anyone to pair with. I had also never been 'on a run' before, and there were boys there who were in the year above me, and I dreaded how embarrassing it was going to be when I got out of breath and would have to stop. We picked up the pace; I found that although I was out of breath and having to work hard, I enjoyed it. I was tired, and it hurt a bit, but I didn't *have* to stop. I could keep up with the older boys. All that bike-riding and roller-blading around the estate had obviously given me some level of fitness. I liked running. I stuck with it.

The next spring, one afternoon after school, Rob, who was a football mad sports enthusiast, said I could go for a run with him to the shop to get some milk. Mum was on a shift selling perfume at Gatwick airport and my brother was absorbed in PlayStation games at his friend's house. We ran into Wokingham town centre, which was the furthest I'd ever run before. On the way back, with

Rob carrying the milk in his backpack, we headed up the long, slow, unrelenting hill from Norreys Avenue to Keep Hatch Farm. The sun was baking on my skin, a sheen of sweat forming on my arms.

The hill was never ending. 'I can't do it,' I said to Rob. 'Yes you can,' he said. 'This is the moment when you decide whether you want to be a runner, or a very good runner.' I let the words sink in, and I knew that I wanted to be a very good runner. In some ways, I knew that it wasn't about running, it was about not giving up on myself. I ran home as fast as I could, and I never forgot that moment. The moment I decided that when things got hard in life, I wouldn't give up. It was my first life lesson.

I was obsessed with running. I loved how it made me feel – light and fast, my lungs and heart pumping blood and oxygen like the pistons of a steam train. I loved going for runs on summer evenings with Rob, while Mum cleared up after dinner. These runs felt like epic adventures at the time, but were probably no longer than half an hour. Rob taught me to always run towards the traffic. He would take me on the country roads behind Wokingham, past farms and huge houses with tennis courts. I remember the peacefulness and how beautiful the countryside looked in the evening light. That was the best thing about running – getting outside and appreciating nature. To me, going on a run was the closest I got to that feeling of wonder.

Actually, the best thing about running was being faster than the boys. Mrs Merrick was our teacher in Year Six at Keep Hatch Junior School; she had also taught Rob when he had been at the same school twenty years earlier. She would start a PE lesson by sending us running around the school perimeter, which was probably about 800 metres. Thirty of us boys and girls would stampede off, sprinting for the fence, the boys always leading the pack. I was never told to, but I knew not to go off too fast. I had seen it on TV – the athlete winning the race would always sit halfway down the field, and then sprint to the finish, overtaking the leaders. The leaders never won – I couldn't understand why they never learnt that. Mrs Merrick would blow her whistle, and the entire class would leave me for dust, but I had learned what my running style was – I wasn't a sprinter; I would be faster towards the end. By the time we were on the final straight, I would always be taking over the last of the boys, and fly into Mrs Merrick who would announce to the class, 'I knew Bonnie was going to beat you all – you all run off too fast!'

We had regular competition evenings at Bracknell Athletic Club. Not that any of the events ever felt competitive, though. We would be lined up and made to jump in the sandpit or throw shot puts. All I was interested in was being in the clubhouse (a dilapidated old Portakabin) afterwards and getting to eat sweets ('white mice' and 'fried eggs') while the medallists in each event were read out. I always came third, and had medal after medal with its red sash. Second place had a blue sash, and first place was yellow. After one event, it was announced that the next competition would be 'long distance', which for us Under-13s meant racing 1,000 metres around the track, all ages against each other.

The boys at the track were much bigger than the boys at school. Some of them were in Year Seven or Eight, and they loved athletics club for the sprinting. I didn't like sprinting. I could never get my arms and legs moving fast enough, and would always come last. But 1,000 metres: that was a distance I knew I should do well in, and Rob knew it too.

Rob decided he was going to train me for the race. He volunteered at the club alongside the two regular ladies. Once they told him off when we all went out for a long run. He pushed me to go faster and faster, until we'd completely lost the group and arrived back at the club-house fifteen minutes before everyone else. I was surprised by how much faster we'd gone. I didn't know whether I was fitter than my peers. I didn't think I was. If they were pushed, I was sure they could run as fast. So why were the volunteers holding them back? It was the first time I thought about how the people around you can affect your potential. I loved the volunteers and knew they gave up their time for free, but perhaps that alone wasn't enough.

Rob took me for an extra session at the track that Sunday, where we did sprint work. I remember leaving the track feeling disappointed, and I could tell Rob was too. I was too slow at sprinting, and Rob knew it would be a fast race against the older boys. Neither of us had much faith in me getting a medal.

Tuesday came, the day of the race. We arrived at the track early and I remember feeling sick. It was the first time in my life I'd felt this kind of nerves. My brother Harry had come along too. I was jealous of him, eating sweets and getting to watch without a care in the world. *I'll never compete again*, I told myself. I would do this one race and retire.

We did some other competitions first – the usual long jump or high jump, which I tried to focus on, but out of the corner of my eye I could see the start line for the 1,000 metres and, as much as I tried, I couldn't think of anything else.

The moment came when the volunteers ushered us over to the start line. For the first time ever, they were even using a starting gun – the pressure couldn't get any worse! I was sure as soon as I heard that gunshot I would have a heart attack, my little heart must have been racing so fast from the nerves and adrenaline. I knew Rob's heart would be in his mouth too – the stands were on the other side of the track, and I knew he would be anxiously watching while my brother chewed on a strawberry shoelace.

The gun went. All thirty of us burst forward and I was instantly left behind. *Should I just go for it*, I thought, *and stick with the pack?* Something told me not to. Ten seconds into the race, I was in last place. Rob was indeed anxiously watching from the stand, thinking the worst. 'She's gone too slow,' he said to my brother, resigning himself to the realisation that all those training sessions had been wasted.

When the pack left me behind, I knew that I needed to stay calm and run my own race. I was obsessed with Billie Piper at the time and, to distract myself, I kept singing the lyrics to her song 'Because We Want To'. Every time I looked up and saw the leaders way out in front I had to stop myself from second-guessing. *Run your own race*, I told myself.

At 300 metres I started overtaking the first stragglers, and with every stride my hips and chest opened out, my shoulders relaxed, I felt stronger and faster. By the time we'd hit the first lap, I was coming up to the leading pack, I could see the oldest boys at the front, and their body language said they'd had enough. I passed the last of them at the 600-metre mark, right in front of the stands. At this point, Rob was on his feet screaming encouragement as I passed, but then had a sinking feeling. 'She's gone too fast,' he said to my brother, still chewing on that strawberry shoelace.

It was the last lap, and as I hit 700 metres I could see to the other side of the track and the rest of the group. I told myself not to get excited, I sang 'Because We Want To' to myself and, finally, at 800 metres, I knew it was time to stop strategising my pace, and just run as fast as I could to the finish line. I threw myself into every stride, lapping the stragglers at the back, and came on to the home straight, where one of the volunteers was screaming at me. I ran straight into her arms and she gave me the tightest hug. She seemed so shocked and overwhelmed. I thought I must have done quite well to have made her this happy. My time was 4 minutes and 3 seconds.

As we drove home, me sitting in the front with my bag of sweets and the medal with the yellow sash around my neck, Rob was going through every nail-biting moment of the race. 'I thought after our training session you wouldn't have a chance against the older boys, then I thought you started too slow, then went too fast! But you knew what you were doing; you ran your own race. I can't believe it. I can't wait to tell your mother. I knew you could do it!'

At that time in my life, if you had asked me what I wanted to do when I grew up, I would have told you that I wanted to win a gold medal at the Olympics. The problem, though, was the fact that I dreaded competing. Not long after winning that race, Bracknell Athletic Club told my parents I had to leave. They had started putting me forward to compete for the club, but on race days I would vomit from the nerves and refuse to compete. It was too much, and just as I started secondary school, I hung up my running trainers, and that was my love of running and of sport done for years.

I had the potential, and who knows where I would have ended up. I love watching the Olympics now, and when I see the Amazonian women line up for the start of the 1,500 metres, which I'm sure would have been my distance, I always get a pang of 'What if?' What if I hadn't let my anxieties beat me? But, my fear of competition was just part of who I was. I put a huge amount of pressure on myself to perform, and these anxieties were just the start of my tumultuous teenage years.

Perhaps life today could have been very different if I had carried on competing. Maybe I would have won a gold medal at the Olympics. Maybe I wouldn't have climbed Everest. We all have 'sliding doors' moments, when one decision can change the course of your life completely. It's mind-boggling if you think about it too much. I like to think that as long as we throw ourselves into making the most of our path in life, we can't go too far wrong. There is a great quote that floats around social media and often appears on my Instagram feed. 'Never half-arse anything. Always use your full arse.' There are so many 'What ifs?' in life, but if you know you've fully committed to your path, and done your best, you shouldn't look back in regret. Who knows, perhaps there's a parallel universe where you took that other path and are living out a completely different life. Now *that's* mind-boggling.

By the time I was aged thirteen, I lived with my mum, my stepdad Rob and my two younger brothers Harry and Alfie in a house on Barkham Road, on the other side of Wokingham to our old estate. One day Mum brought home two cats, which she named Tinkerbell and Bubbles. My brother Harry and I split our time between Mum's place in Wokingham and our dad's house in Bracknell.

At my dad's we had five more siblings: Oli, Ben, Sean, Emily and Olivia. So in total, there were eight of us kids. And I was the oldest. Both my dad and my stepdad run their own businesses, and I've grown up exposed to their entrepreneurial spirit, but also the uncertainty and responsibility of not having a monthly pay cheque. My dad and stepdad showed me from a young age to take responsibility for my future. 'If you want something in life, you go out there and find a way to make it happen,' my dad said to me once as I sat in the dusty cab of his truck, surrounded by hard hats and high-vis jackets.

When I think of my stepdad, I think of him being at his desk in our study every morning, often before 5 a.m. He would tease me and my brothers that he'd already done a day's work by the time we woke up. Their philosophy was simple – you can do anything if you work hard.

My mum worked too, at the airport selling perfume and then eventually for my stepdad when his business took off. My wider family are also from self-employed stock – my nan built up a hairdressing business in the 1970s and still runs her shop in Godalming today. A lot of my family went into the hairdressing trade or the building trade. Overall, there are only a few of us that are not self-employed. So it comes as no surprise that my brothers and I have followed suit – they are also in the building trade, while I pursued mountaineering.

My parents were a constant but subconscious inspiration throughout my life. They led by example and never pushed or forced me to be an over-achieving teenager. My dad would happily drive me to different clubs and pay for ski holidays, and my stepdad obviously took me under his wing when I was at the athletics club, but I never felt pushed. In fact, my brothers and I often joke that we were mostly left to our own decisions and devices, which is probably why we are all so independent-minded. We saw our parents getting on with things, watched their successes, and realised that it was all down to hard work.

I once berated my mum for not pushing me harder. 'I could have done so well at school if you'd have made me do my homework!'

'Bonnie,' she'd say, giving me one of her looks, 'according to you, you'd always done it already!' That was probably the problem: I imagine I was lying to Mum to avoid doing the work; I was certainly always the person at school who handed homework in late, and I did terribly at my GCSEs compared to my friends. My parents would joke that I was the black sheep of the family. I was content to read my books (*Harry Potter*, *His Dark Materials*, *The Wind on Fire* trilogy) and I had weird obsessions with dinosaurs and the movie *Jurassic Park*. My family are very sociable and loved family gatherings. I liked my own company.

As much as they were inspiring to grow up around in

the sense of their work ethic, my family will be the first to admit that they had limiting beliefs. I told my stepdad I wanted to be a movie director when I was about ten years old, and he told me it was too late, that directors like Steven Spielberg would have been making movies since they were 'about five'. My family believed that you got a job and you worked hard, and you never left Wokingham, but you got a bigger house and a nicer car than your parents' generation. My generation was different. I went to an all-girls' secondary school, and I remember in assemblies being told by the teachers: 'Girls, you can do anything you want in life. Anything at all.' I wasn't interested in staying in Wokingham when I grew up; I wanted to escape. I didn't know where to or what I would do, but I knew I wanted to see the world.

One afternoon my stepdad picked us up from school and I announced in the car that one day I was going to climb Mount Everest. I must have been about sixteen at the time. 'Don't be ridiculous, Bonnie, you have to be super-human to climb Everest.' And that was the end of the conversation. For all of my parents' amazing attitudes towards going far in life, they never wanted to think *too* far outside the box.

But Rob was right: did I really want to climb Mount Everest? I'd never climbed a mountain. We'd never been to North Wales or the Lake District. The reason I had said it was because my geography teacher had talked about people climbing Everest in her lesson that day, and I had found myself sitting there and thinking:

'I think I'd be quite good at that.'

CHAPTER 3

Just get it over with, I told myself as I pushed two fingers to the back of my throat. I was kneeling on the cold, hard tiles of the family bathroom floor, my head in the toilet bowl. I finally retched, and the strain caused a rush of blood to my head. I could feel the pressure building behind my eyes.

I flushed the toilet and pulled myself off the floor. Splashing some water over my face, I caught my reflection in the mirror: red and swollen skin, bloodshot eyes. It was a demon staring back at me. The weakest and worst possible side of me revealed. I was faced with an undeniable truth: I had absolutely no self-worth, no self-control. *What have I become?*

I pressed a towel into my face and breathed deeply into it. *It's over*, I told myself. The frenzy of a binge and purge is all-consuming, fast-paced, a desperate scramble. This was the calm after the storm, the moment when I would hope upon hope that I could reset, stay strong, and tell myself it would never happen again. Not today at least.

Incredibly, this day was to become one of the most pivotal of my life. Not that I could possibly know that, though, slumped over the bathroom sink in exhaustion, feeling utterly disgusted with myself.

I was seventeen years old. I was drowning.

* * *

Running was a huge part of my life as a kid, and as an adult it is too, but there was a period when I was a teenager when I wasn't running and, during those years from age thirteen to seventeen, like a lot of young women, I struggled with body image and disordered eating.

I saw my athletic, child's body change as I hit puberty. I didn't recognise the voluptuous young woman in the mirror, and that made me feel uneasy and confused.

I was also starting to become more aware of the world around me. I was young, impressionable, and too immature to question the messaging that emanates constantly from advertising and the media. Every day, from the TV to the bus stop, I saw images and adverts of beautiful, slim and seemingly happy young women. The media were gripped by the 'size zero' fad. I felt overwhelmed by how imperfect I looked in comparison to the perfect beauty that surrounded me. I started to believe that if I wanted to be successful in life, I had to look like the smiling, slim women that beamed at me from the pages of magazines, TV screens and hoardings.

Meanwhile, the diet industry pedalled a simple message – to live life to the full you couldn't be fat. Being fat made you unattractive and unhappy. Their advertising told me that I 'deserved' the body of my dreams. Weight Watchers, Atkins, Special K, SlimFast, and celebrity fitness DVDs showed happy people evangelising about how much better life was now that they were a few pounds lighter. The message was clear – the rewards of being thin were far-reaching and life-changing. To be fat was to hold yourself back.

As I hit my teens, I began to fear putting on weight.

These fears outweighed my every waking thought and, over time, being skinny like the girls in magazines became the most important thing in my life. Not running or sports, not having fun with my friends, but being thin. It seemed as though I had gone to bed one night identifying myself as a sporty and energetic girl who measured life by how much fun she was having, and woke up a teenager who based her worth on being as slim as possible, and measured her life by what number the scales said. I lost so much when that transition happened in my mind, and it was to curse me for many years to come.

I stopped eating breakfast, and then I began to avoid going to the canteen at lunch, with its piles of cupcakes and cookies placed right at the till, cleverly tempting us students to spend more. I would see how far I could get through the school day without eating anything at all. I realised that I could go all day and make it back home from school at 4 p.m. without eating a single bite of food. I remember walking home from school and feeling the ground rush towards me – I was so low on energy, I was on the verge of fainting.

I became a nightmare teenager. I was always exhausted, tired and irritable. I was hungry all the time, and found myself thinking about food constantly. I found it hard to concentrate at school. I thought that this was my personality; that it was normal to feel so disengaged. I couldn't understand why my classmates seemed to learn faster than me, why everyone around me had more energy, was laughing more, having more fun. I thought it was just me.

I spent lesson after lesson – for over a year – just clock-watching until the end of the day. I was so hungry and so distracted by my empty stomach, all I could think about was the moment I would come through the door at home and finally have a huge bowl of cereal – always Special K with red berries with a mountain of Canderel sweetener on top. Diet food. Food I had been told was 'acceptable'.

My mum was exasperated with me. I was dreadful to be around, and once, after another struggle over me not wanting to eat the dinner she had cooked, she asked me, 'Are you on a diet? Just tell me the truth!' I lied and said no. Afterwards, I questioned why I had said no. Why was I so ashamed to be on a diet? Why didn't I just say yes and have a conversation with my mum openly about it? I never shared how I felt, not even with my school friends. I felt isolated and gripped by my obsessions with dieting and food, but then again, I was now aged fifteen: isn't this supposed to be what life's like when you're fifteen?

One evening, after eating too much dinner, the all-too-familiar feeling of wishing away the fat and calories came over me. I dreaded what the scales would say in the morning. I desperately wished for a way to rectify my lapse in control. Then an idea popped into my head: *Why don't you make yourself sick?*

I went upstairs to the bathroom and forced my fingers down my throat. When I was actually sick, I was surprised and shocked. Then, there was a moment of euphoria – I had cheated the system. I had gorged myself on dinner, and now wouldn't even have to suffer the consequences or the wretched guilt that came with eating.

After that, I thought I had discovered the secret that everyone in the world wanted to know: I could eat any food I wanted and never had to worry about gaining weight.

It was like magic. For a while I relaxed my strict eating habits and allowed myself to enjoy more food, only to disappear to the bathroom afterwards to vomit it back up. For the first time in years, I felt relaxed around food and yet still in control. But, slowly, I went from the one being in control, to being controlled.

By the time I realised what was happening, it was already too late. After depriving myself so much for two years, the pendulum had swung back in the other direction and I had started to get uncontrollable urges to binge-eat. I felt as though I had a parasite in my head, ravaging my ability to think straight, make decisions, or do anything other than indulge in out-of-control binge-eating followed by making myself sick afterwards.

These urges to binge and purge started with a 'switch' in my head: as soon as the switch went, I became powerless to reason and powerless to fight. There wasn't a particular trigger for the switch like stress or anxiety. It felt more like a glitch in a computer programme: my brain wanted to repeat the same destructive behaviour over and over for no obvious reason, and despite how much I hated it. No matter how much I didn't want to start the cycle of bingeing and purging, nothing I could say or do would stop me. I was possessed.

Bulimia took over my life, in a much more distressing and dangerous way than my dieting ever did. I stopped clock-watching during lessons and instead became terrified of the after-school hours when the urges would raise their ugly voices. I had become a prisoner in my own mind.

By the time I turned seventeen in 2005 I had suffered from bulimia for two years and was desperately out of control. I had put on nearly two stone in weight, and every part of my life was suffering – from my GCSE results to my friendships.

I had tried so hard to stop, but I was so ashamed by what I was doing that I couldn't bring myself to reach out to anyone. I wanted so desperately to make a change. To just be *normal*. I would think back to how I was as a young girl, so full of energy and life and self-assured. *What had happened to her?*

Over and over, I would tell myself I would be strong enough to fight the urges *next time*; that I would get myself better. I never managed to. I was at a loss and fighting a battle that nobody knew about.

And then, in the middle of the Easter holidays in my first year of sixth form, I finally found myself in the bathroom on the day that changed my life.

It won't happen again, I tried to promise myself as I stared at the bloodshot reflection in the mirror.

It was the third time I had made myself sick that day, a new record. I couldn't see how I could take any more. The next urge to start bingeing and purging was probably hours away. Perhaps there would be more after that. I was terrified of these urges, and for the first time I found myself accepting that they were more powerful than me. They controlled me. I had no choice but to give in. I had no energy left to fight. I had never felt such helplessness.

You'll never get over this.

I quietly left the bathroom and went back downstairs into the study. I sat down in front of the family computer and stared blankly at the screen, thinking about how I was going to get through the rest of the day without succumbing to the next urge. I just wanted the hours to pass quickly so that the day would be over. The amount of hours left until bedtime made my anxious heart race.

I logged on to the computer and into my email account. I never really received emails, but a few days earlier, in desperation, I had sent an email to an eating disorder specialist after reading an article about him in a magazine. When I had pressed the send button I had felt for a moment as if there might be a way out. A flicker of hope. *Maybe he'll be able to save me.* That feeling had been fleeting, though. After sending that email, I had gone straight back to my old ways.

To my amazement, there was an email from the doctor. I held my breath. *What if my mum sees this?* I thought, then: *This is it. This man is going to make me better.*

I opened the email to find that it had been written by his assistant:

'Thank you for your email. You can make an appointment with the doctor in Bristol next month. His fees start at £200 an hour ...'

I felt crushed. Going to see him was impossible. I would never be able to find £200, or go to Bristol by myself. It is no exaggeration to say that whatever strength I had left was wiped out in that moment. My last hope was gone. For the first time since my problems with eating started, I felt tears stain my cheeks. I tasted the salt on my lips. I sobbed into my hands in despair.

As I cried, I thought about the fact that I would probably never get to live a normal life. I felt as if I was stuck at the bottom of a dark hole. I could look up and see the world, a world full of light, a world that 'normal' people – my friends and everyone else – seemed to inhabit. But not me. I was stuck in the dark with my demons and I couldn't find a way out. I just wanted to be *normal*. Something that everyone else took for granted was impossible for me.

If only the doctor and his assistant knew how trapped I was, how desperately I needed help. I couldn't believe that they didn't seem to care about the struggle I was going through. Didn't they know how desperately I wanted to just be normal?

It's not up to them to make you normal. It's up to you.

There it was. With that thought, my tears stopped. Silence filled the room. A realisation washed through me, and suddenly, with total clarity, I understood.

It's not up to them to make you normal. It's up to you.

No doctor, no psychotherapist, no other person on this planet was going to be able to wave a magic wand and give me what I wanted. If I wanted to be normal, it was up to me.

I have to stop being a victim and take responsibility for myself.

It seems like the most obvious thought in the world, but I had to hit rock bottom to see it. Everything suddenly made sense. It wasn't my fault that I had an eating disorder, but it was my responsibility to reclaim my life; nobody else could do that for me. If I wanted to be normal, it was up to me.

Unlike the millions of other times I told myself I would get myself better, this felt different. I felt as if I could distinguish two different people in my mind. There was the real me, the person I was in that moment who wanted desperately to get better, who was feeling ashamed and confused and scared. Then, there were these animalistic demons that I was terrified of, who took over my mind at the flick of a 'switch' and convinced me over and over to drop everything I was doing and follow their orders to binge and purge. The real me had become no match for my internal demons' powers of persuasion.

I knew with such clarity that if the real me was at rock bottom, then my chances of standing up to these demons were even smaller. Every time I felt ashamed or guilty or upset, I was giving the urges in my brain a better chance of convincing me to do as they told me. I realised that if I felt like a victim, then I would continue to be treated like one. I had to stop being a victim, and build up the person who was going to have to fight these demons. I had to do something, anything, that would empower the real me, so that I could stand up for myself. And I knew I couldn't wait, as it wouldn't be long before the demons would raise their ugly heads again, and the real me would be lost once more.

In a moment of pure serendipity, I turned around in my chair to see the old treadmill stacked up in the corner of the study. It was gathering dust and obscured by piles of books and files. It had been there for years and I had never taken any notice of it, but now, for some reason, it seemed like the perfect way to make a stand against the demons in my mind.

Get on the treadmill.

I hadn't run a single step in years. I knew it was going to be the shortest run in history. But I didn't care. I had to do it. I *had to.*

For so long, I had been beaten down and not fought back. Now I was fighting – just a meagre swipe – but I had to *start*, to show myself that I was not going to be a victim any more.

I got up, pulled away the stacks of books, pushed the plug into the wall and wiped the dust off the console. I pressed 'Start' and the treadmill chugged into life. I wasn't in exercise clothes, or a sports bra. I didn't even have any shoes on.

As I stepped on to the treadmill, I told myself that it didn't matter how long I ran for, *anything* was an achievement. *This is for me.* I pushed the buttons until I was forced to break into a jog, then a run, and finally a near sprint. My heart pounded, I felt a tightness in my chest as I gasped for oxygen. My legs seared with the build-up of lactic acid. *I am so unfit!* I scrambled for the 'Off' button while hanging on to the safety bar. The treadmill slowed and came to a stop. I looked at the timer – 46 seconds.

I stood there, huffing and puffing, staring at the timer: 46 seconds. *Nothing and everything.*

A gut feeling told me that that moment was the first step in a huge journey. After so much angst and pain, it took just 46 seconds to change my life.

Today, I can push my body through extreme physical pain for hours, if not days, when I am climbing the world's highest peaks. Forty-six seconds? Absolutely nothing. But, that moment was the start of my journey to Everest in some ways. It was the beginning of a new mind-set, a mind-set that in the future would lead me to take on seemingly impossible challenges and to push myself to try things that I was almost bound to fail at. That moment gave me the attitude that has affected every major decision in my life ever since.

In that moment I realised that it didn't matter how sad I felt, how lost or how victimised I was: nobody had as much to gain or lose when it came to my own life as I did. Ultimately, whatever shit I had been through, it didn't matter whose fault it was – I was the one who had to pick up the pieces. Nobody else could do that for me. My life, my happiness, rested on my shoulders alone. No ifs and buts. The buck stopped with me.

It dawned on me that I could either let these urges in my brain continue to control and eventually ruin my life, or I could see them for what they were – as destructive and unwelcome, and not a part of the person that I knew in my heart I was. The real me had hopes and dreams; the real me laughed with her friends, felt love and gratitude, and also pain and sadness too. These demons didn't feel or care about anything – they were not me at all.

I had to do things that nourished the *real* me. If she was strong, she would be better able to dismiss the demons clouding her mind. It sounds far too simplistic but, in that moment as I stepped on to that treadmill, I knew in my heart I was making a simple choice. We can choose to be victims, or we can choose to be responsible for our own happiness in life. Regardless of what has happened to us, and in spite of what has happened to us, we choose how to act. Life is not fair, and often things that happen to us are not our fault. We have to try and make the best of our lives, and that choice – to make the most of life – is ours alone to make.

Those 46 life-changing seconds weren't about calories burned or distance or speed. It was something much more important. Those seconds showed me that I had always had the power in my hands to change my life. And that it wasn't up to my future self to solve my problems; it was a power I had in my hands right there and then, so what was I waiting for?

It sounds ludicrous after having battled for so long with bulimia, but after that first run I was pretty much cured. The urges disappeared almost completely after those 46 seconds. I don't know why, but after doing something that seemed to be positive, I didn't get the urge to binge-eat, or make myself sick. I didn't want to. Quite simply, the urges stopped and I went back to normal.

At the time of writing this, twelve years on, I have had a few relapses, but I have been totally free of bulimia for a long time now, and while the demons do appear some-times, they are weak by comparison to the real me that dominates my mind. Sometimes I find myself wondering how on earth I ever gave in to such urges. It is at moments like that that I have to stop myself and take stock of how far I've come since that day on the bathroom floor.

I both do and don't regret what I went through. I think about the needless angst and wasted years I inflicted on myself, and I'm angry that I let society and the media shape how I thought about and treated myself. I wonder what my life would be like now if I had never succumbed to my insecurities and had instead invested my energies in the things that had made me happy as a kid – namely running and being outdoors. Then again, coming out the other side

40

of such a dark time shaped my attitude to life and showed me what was possible when I chose to act. Therefore, my eating disorder has truly shaped who I am. If I had not gone through this period as an anxious teenager, then would I have pushed myself to do such extreme challenges later on? I will never know the answer to that question; all I can do is try to make sense of my past and try to learn lessons to take with me through life.

Running from that day onwards became part of my life again, and has been ever since. For me, just the simplicity of movement – stride after stride, chest and hips open, arms beating back and forth, deep breaths of precious air – feels so natural and so right.

After those 46 seconds, I went back to the treadmill the next day and ran for 1 minute. I told myself that it was progress, and better than nothing. I was determined to become a runner again and prove to myself that I could do this own my own. I built up to 15 minutes on the tread-mill over the next few weeks, and I stuck at it every day, mainly because I didn't set any outlandish goals or pressure myself too much. I just took every single second as a victory against the dark hole I'd been in a few weeks earlier.

A year later, I crossed the finish line of the 2006 Reading Half Marathon. Rob was there waiting for me. He had run it too. I had done it in 2 hours and 12 minutes. Not exactly the incredible time I'd set in my 1,000-metre race all those years before, but it didn't matter. I had come a long way since that 46-second run – not just in my running mileage, but in every aspect of my life. I found that doing something that connected me with my body – my heart, my lungs, my muscles – made me want to look after myself. I started to think of my body as a tool to help me get the most out of life, not as something to manipulate into looking a certain way for the sake of others.

Two years later, when I was nineteen years old, I was training to run the 2008 London Marathon. I loved the head-space that running gave me, so the longer I ran for, the better. A marathon seemed like the perfect challenge to sink my teeth into.

I would regularly run 16 miles from my university to my mum's house, turning up on the doorstep unannounced at 9 o'clock at night, nothing with me but the sweaty clothes I was wearing. The next day I'd either persuade my mum to drive me back to campus, or get the train wearing one of her jackets.

One weekend at home, I was on a long run and hoped to clock about 18 miles, and midway through I decided to detour to Bracknell Athletic Club. The club looked just the same as I remembered it – ramshackle and rough around the edges. I ran through the gate and on to the red 400-metre track. I don't know why, but I felt tears in my eyes. After all this time, I had finally rediscovered what truly made me happy. I ran back home feeling as though I had come full circle, and now, with the marathon to look forward to, I was picking up where I had quit at that track all those years before.

As I ran home, I thought a lot about the journey I was on. I was discovering so much about myself that had been lost to calorie-counting and obsessing over the scales, like the fact that I was far more capable of overcoming challenges than I believed possible. I started to think: *If I can get myself out of a black hole like that, what else am I capable of?*

I thought about the importance of taking even the smallest step as a victory, because each one builds upon the last. That 46-second run had built up to me now training for a marathon, and while I didn't know it yet, in years to come would turn into 30-hour marathon climbs in the death zone. Whenever I'm having a great run, I feel so glad I started taking those first small steps on that day when I hit rock bottom. I'm so glad that I didn't leave that responsibility to make a change to my future self.

Finding running helped me realise that humans need purpose, we need direction and to seek fulfilment. Now I had started pushing myself, I began to believe that the sky was the limit.

CHAPTER 4

Rain splattered the pavement. The puddles shimmered yellow and red under the traffic lights, splashing our legs as we ran as fast as we could along Kensington Gore, past the Science Museum up towards Hyde Park. A friend from university, Meghan, and I were on our way to Number 1 Kensington Gore, which housed the Royal Geographical Society, and we were late.

Breathless and sodden, we arrived at the hallowed building, where explorers have congregated for nearly 200 years. The reception was brightly lit and starkly modern. The din of chatter reverberated off the glass walls and glossy floors. It was packed with people holding glasses of cheap wine, stubborn raindrops clinging to their coats.

Just as we came through the door, an announcement came through the address system that the lecture was about to start. The hordes of black coats filed towards the famous Ondaatje Theatre. Meghan and I jostled our way in and squeezed on to one of the long benches, nodding and smiling at the eager-looking people either side of us.

I wasn't really sure why I was there, and I was sure Meghan wasn't either. It was late September in 2008 and we were in our final year of university at Royal Holloway, she studying Social Care and me Media Arts. I had finished the London Marathon a few months earlier. For some reason we had decided to travel up especially from Egham to South Kensington to spend our evening listening to a lecture about climbing mountains.

Why? Who knows? 'Maybe there'll be some hot guys there,' we had joked, but in all honesty, neither of us knew anything about mountains, or were on the look-out for potential dates. I was cursing myself as we sat down on one of the tightly packed benches, thinking that the evening was going to be a waste of time, but then I stopped myself and thought: *What's the worst that can happen?*

The lecture was entitled 'Blood, Sweat and Frozen Tears on the World's Highest Peak'. It was to be presented by two people I'd never heard of: Rob Casserley and Kenton Cool.

On stage was a state-of-the-art Mountain Hardwear expedition tent and a mannequin wearing an 8,000-metre-peak down suit made by The North Face, with a pair of goggles and what looked like a fighter pilot's mask. It looked like an astronaut. The stage was bathed in warm yellow light and, having just come in from the rain, it felt like settling down in front of a glowing fire.

Dark wood panels lined the walls of the theatre, each carved with the name of a legendary explorer: Young, Husband, Scott, Shackleton, Hillary; the reams of names went on and on, panel after panel around the room. The eccentric history of the RGS was all around us, the expeditions of old meeting the cutting-edge and new. I could imagine the great pioneers of exploration and what they might have looked like. It felt as if they were still here. I couldn't understand why, but a certain feeling of being 'at home' came over me. This world was so new, and yet I felt a sense of belonging.

The lights came down and the audience started to fizz with excitement, eager for the two mountaineers to transport them with their storytelling to the world's highest peaks. Rob Casserley and Kenton Cool walked on to the stage to a loud round of applause.

Both in their early thirties, Kenton was a British mountain guide living in Chamonix in the French Alps, and fast becoming a celebrity in the UK for his high-profile expeditions for charity and TV. He was tall and wiry, with a chipped front tooth from a rock-climbing accident that had also smashed his ankle some years before.

If Kenton was a mountaineering thoroughbred, with his guiding prestige, then Rob was well … a workhorse. Rob was a full-time GP in Devon, and briefly mentioned at the start of the lecture that his next challenge with his annual leave was to row across the Atlantic Ocean with his housemate. Between them, they had climbed Mount Everest eleven times. And Everest was what they going to tell us about.

At 8,848 metres high, it is the highest peak on the planet. Known in Tibet as Chomolungma, meaning Holy Mother, it was first climbed by Tenzing Norgay and Edmund Hillary from its South East Ridge on the Nepalese side of the mountain. It was believed for many years to be a peak so high that no bird could fly above it. Though, since Norgay and Hillary's ascent on the eve of the Queen's coronation, 10 May 1953, hundreds of climbers had scaled its treacherous glaciers and crumbling walls of rock to the summit.

The two mountaineers told the packed audience how every year they battled up Everest for nearly five weeks, dealing with minus 25°C temperatures, ice storms and knee-deep snow. We hung on their every word. The worst thing, they said, was the altitude. The fact that, with every step higher and higher up the mountain, there was less oxygen for them to breathe, until they stepped above 8,000 metres, and from that point onwards, there was so little oxygen that they described the world up that high as a death zone. Quite simply nothing could survive up there – no plant life, no insects, especially not human beings.

To survive in the death zone, Rob and Kenton described how they used bottled oxygen, and didn't stop for sleep as they climbed to the summit in a mammoth 24-hour push, only stopping at their last camp – Camp Four, or 'death camp', to rest for a few hours before continuing. They described how whether they slept or climbed, their bodies were shutting down, until they would eventually die. They were on a race against time, climbing through one of the most dangerous environments on Earth, their bodies trying to function without sleep, energy from food or able to breathe.

They were super-human. I couldn't imagine going through so much pain. It sounded horrendous. *Why would anyone want to go somewhere where there was no oxygen?*

Finally, they said something that I've never forgotten; when they finally reached the summit of Everest, after all that hard work, they looked down, and beneath them they could see the curvature of the Earth. They were so high up, it was if they were looking down on our planet from space.

I couldn't believe what I had just heard. I had never imagined that something so beautiful existed. They described how they would always try to reach the summit for sunrise, to see the curvature of the Earth illuminated by a bright orange glow. They said the summit was peaceful, desolate, and a place where man could almost touch the heavens. I was spellbound.

Sitting in my chair, surrounded by hundreds of other people in the audience, I said to myself: *One day I have got to climb Mount Everest and I have got to see the curvature of the Earth with my own eyes.*

The lecture finished to rapturous applause. I wished it could have gone on all night. 'Did you like it?' Meghan asked as we were shuffled out of the theatre along with everyone else.

'Loved it,' I said.

I glanced back at the climbing paraphernalia on the stage, and I had an inexplicable feeling. I was going to climb Mount Everest. I knew I was. There was no logical reason that I could put my finger on as to why. It was just as if I'd known it somehow all along.

What a load of absolute rubbish.

I frowned as the sunlight streamed in through my bedroom window, piercing my eyelids and forcing me awake. Mount Everest? *What on Earth was I thinking?*

After a night dreaming about how I was going to scale the world's highest peak, I had woken up to reality. I couldn't believe that, even for a second, I had been considering the idea of climbing the world's highest mountain. *You idiot.* I was so embarrassed. Thank god I hadn't mentioned it to Meghan.

I threw on some clothes, grabbed my bag and headed out for my lectures and workshops in the Media Arts building. Later, sitting in my lecture about French *film noir*, I found myself staring at the ceiling panels and the artificial lights, thinking of what it would be like to be above the clouds, my feet crunching in snow, breathing rarefied air through chapped lips, the Himalayas stretched out beneath me. The professor droned on. Being here in this room suddenly felt so mundane and pointless. As much as I tried to concentrate on what he was saying, I couldn't shake my Everest hangover.

Lying in bed that night, I tried to talk these silly thoughts out of my head. *You've never even climbed a mountain!* My stepdad's words, 'You've got to be super-human to climb Everest' came to mind too. Super-human? I definitely wasn't that. *Best to stop thinking about this, and get on with your life*, I told myself.

I tossed and turned that night, and for many after. I would lie awake thinking about the mountains and wondering how I might ever get to them. I knew it didn't make any sense, and I couldn't give myself one logical reason why I so desperately wanted to become a mountaineer – all the suffering and pain, all the risk and near certainty of failure or death – but logic didn't seem to cut it: there was something more powerful at work; something that was beyond the world of reason. Night after night, I fell asleep dreaming about what it would be like to battle my way up that mountain, giving it everything I had, and be rewarded on the summit with a view of the curvature of the Earth.

One afternoon, a few weeks after the lecture, I found myself writing a 'bucket list', curled up on the sofa with a cup of tea. The movie of the same name had just come

out. I'd never heard the term before, and decided to jump
on the bandwagon and write down a list of things I wanted
to do in my twenties. I wrote down the usual:

- find a job that I love, probably in TV production
- travel the world
- learn to scuba-dive
- learn Spanish
- run a sub 3-hour 30-minute marathon
- climb Mount Everest

I stopped and stared at the ink drying on the page.
Something inside me was serious about this. More serious
than I had thought.

I was shocked reading the words back to myself again.
What was I doing writing Everest down?

No matter how ludicrous and seemingly impossible it
would be to climb Everest, it was there, written among the
goals I wanted to reach by the time I was 30. Each goal
represented a part of my life, and Everest seemed to repre-
sent something that was the most primal of all; it came
from a place I didn't quite understand but felt an overwhelming desire to trust in. I was drawn to it and I didn't
know why. It took me to write it down to recognise just
how strong that gut instinct was.

I went to bed that night and again found myself staring
up at the ceiling as the hours passed. Something was telling
me that this was what I was meant to do. That my path
was laid out for me, and all I had to do was trust in it. I
hadn't had such an overwhelming instinct since the day I
stepped on to that treadmill and knew somehow that I was

cured of my eating disorder. It was the same gut feeling – to trust in a crazy idea, even though it made no logical sense at all.

I longed to get out into the world where maybe I could give Everest a real shot, but even when I had finished my degree, even though I felt so strongly that I needed to do this, I still didn't have a clue where to begin.

That was what played over and over in my mind the most. How could I start a journey I knew so little about?

I thought about the two mountaineers, Rob and Kenton, who had given the lecture at the RGS. I was so jealous of them. How lucky were they to have stood where they'd stood?

As soon as the word 'lucky' came into my head, the words of my dad and my stepdad interrupted: 'There's no such thing as luck, it's just hard work.' I thought about it for a second. My dads were right: these mountaineers weren't lucky; they were normal people just like me, who had been fortunate enough to stumble upon a passion for climbing.

The more I thought about it, it became obvious. Nobody is born an expert; even the best climbers in the world must have been beginners like me at some point. They too would have been wondering how to take their very first step.

The fundamental difference between them and me was not that they were lucky or talented or super-human. It was that they'd *started*.

I hadn't. I had spent the last few months fretting and worrying and convincing myself with every reason possible that this was a silly idea and doomed to fail. I had done a lot of thinking, but that amounted to nothing. I needed to stop thinking and just *start*.

Everything came back to taking that innocent first step, just like I had learnt the day I chose to step on to that treadmill. *Anything is better than nothing.*

Maybe my first step didn't even have to be climbing; maybe it was something even smaller. The only thing I could think to do was to ask someone else what I should do. I made a promise to myself there and then that the next morning I would do *something* towards my goal of climbing Everest.

The next morning I woke up to the familiar silence of my bedroom. The night before had seemed so full of excitement, my imagination whirring like a film projecting light into the darkness.

This morning felt different somehow. I didn't wake up and curse myself for wasting my time thinking about Everest again. I sat on the edge of my bed and remembered what I'd concluded the night before: *Even the greatest mountaineers have had to start from somewhere. The difference between them and you is that they started.*

A line from the famous poem 'The Road Not Taken' by Robert Frost popped into my mind:

Two roads diverged in a wood, and I,
I took the one less traveled by,
And that has made all the difference

As I sat there, about to take the first step into the day, I could see two roads laid out in front of me. I knew I could either let this day become like every other, just another day that I would probably never remember, or this could be the day when I could start. This could be the first day of the rest of my life.

I told myself that even if I did do something, it would probably never come to anything anyway. But maybe, just maybe, it might.

So, that morning I decided that I would message Rob Casserley and Kenton Cool on Facebook and ask them for advice on how to start climbing. I got up and switched on my laptop. That moment, right there, as I started typing away, was the most important moment on this whole journey. It was the moment that I gave the crazy idea in my head a chance.

As I pressed the send button I thought, *Probably nothing will come of that*. But it didn't matter. There was no pressure; it was just an innocent message asking for advice.

Within a few minutes, my inbox pinged – it was a message from Kenton Cool.

I met Kenton about a week later at King Cross Station. It was a crisp October morning morning in the middle of rush hour. I should have been at lectures, but here I was, embarked on a road, not sure where it was leading, or whether I should even be taking it.

'It's all about stepping stones,' he said as we sat in a café sipping coffee, commuters rushing past us. 'To attempt Everest you need to be an experienced Himalayan climber, and to be an experienced Himalayan climber you need to be an experienced Alpine climber, and to be experienced there, you need to be a good Scottish winter climber, and to be experienced there, you need to have a good base of skills in rope work, climbing technique, team work, and that comes from getting outdoors every weekend and going climbing on small hills, rock climbs, anything and everything. Everest is about milestones, and remembering that all the steps you take, from the first to the last, are all interlinked.'

'So, there is a clear path then, that I could take? I don't need to be super-human?'

'Bonita, you don't need to have the fitness levels of an Olympic athlete. You need experience. Hours built up in the hills, training your body and mind to be resilient, so that one day you'll be able to climb in the death zone ... And you need to want it really badly – climbing Everest is not easy. I see people all the time who tell me they want to climb Everest ... ninety-nine per cent of them never do. You need to have that spark, that passion, otherwise you won't stay committed when things get tough.'

I listened and thought: *I don't want to be the ninety-nine per cent*.

'Remember, no step is too small. Just get out there, join a climbing club – even if it's an indoor wall, it's a place to start. And keep at it; if you stay committed you will progress and, before you know it, you'll be climbing Everest with me and my team.'

I couldn't quite believe what I was hearing. Somehow, a week ago, I'd been lying in bed convinced Everest was impossible, and now here I was having coffee with an Everest legend, who was telling me in the most matter-of-fact way that one day I might climb to the top of the world with his team.

Just as Kenton was about to leave for his train, I asked him one last question. 'What's next for you then, now you've climbed the world's highest mountain?'

'I'd say Lhotse and Nuptse followed by Everest in one single push.'

I looked at Kenton, feeling he had lived up to my assumptions: he really *was* super-human.

From the stuff I'd learnt online, Lhotse was the world's fourth highest peak, and more people had stood on the Moon than had stood on the summit of Nuptse. These two mountains had formidable reputations, and were rarely climbed. They joined together with Everest in a ridge formation to make up what was known as the Everest Horseshoe. Most climbers who reached the summit of Everest never went back to attempt those two mysterious and lesser-known mountains. Lhotse and Nuptse were the largely forgotten ugly sisters to Everest. Kenton was surely unhinged.

With that, in a whirlwind of a yellow rucksacks and a red down jacket, Kenton was diving out of the café and into the morning crush. I sat for a moment as he disappeared into a sea of grey suits, and I realised I was smiling to myself. I had learnt so much and yet none of it seemed overwhelming. *Maybe it was possible.*

CHAPTER 5

I lived in a house just on the edge of Royal Holloway campus with my three close friends Jo, Lucy and Sophie. We spoke to each other mostly in Bridget Jones quotes. 'Where the fuck's the fucking tuna?' was a particular favourite. Vegetarian Domino's pizzas were ordered at least twice a week. And we were convinced that we had invented a drink that we called Squashka: orange squash with water, topped with a double shot of Tesco vodka. As you can probably guess, we weren't great with managing our money; most of our student loan instalments were spent in Primark within the first week of term.

I had told the girls about my plan to climb Everest, and Jo, who was always honest with me, raised an eyebrow.

'What?' I said when I saw her face.

'Bon, you say you're going to do something like this every week!'

Jo was right. I was always coming up with silly ideas, the last one being that I wanted to go to Mongolia and work as a trainee news anchor. Jo smiled awkwardly as if to say 'How can we take this seriously?' and the girls teased me like friends do.

But, Jo and Lucy had always gone out of their way to be supportive friends. They had been there at the finish line of the London Marathon, and had put me to bed that night with a bowl of Ben and Jerry's ice cream and pillows to prop up my swollen feet. When they knew I was serious about something, they would do whatever they could to help out. But Everest was different. 'This is just insane, Bon!' they would plead with me, when I told them about meeting up with Kenton or bored them with Everest stories I'd read online. They thought that my chances of ever making it even to the bottom of that peak were zero. 'People like us don't climb mountains like Everest!'

Seeing how incredulous they were was another kick of motivation that I needed, and encouraged by my meeting with Kenton a few days before, I booked Lucy and myself on to a taster session at the local climbing wall and vowed to prove to my girls just how serious I was.

A few days later, we were at Craggy Island in Guildford. I was dressed in my Lycra and running shoes, and struggling to put on a rather unattractive fabric harness. Lucy and I giggled at how silly we thought we looked, and nervously waited for our turn to climb the brightly coloured resin holds to the top of the 12-metre-high wall.

During the taster session, the first thing we were taught was how to tie a figure-of-eight knot. As the instructor looped the rope around itself, I watched intently and could instantly remember how to do it. Since that first climb, I've always had a knack of being able to learn knots really quickly, a skill that would be vital later on in the hills.

Lucy was shown how to attach the rope to a belay device, and clip it correctly to her harness with a screwgate karabiner. I was attached to the other end of the rope via the knot I'd tied. Lu pulled the rope tight, and the instructor nodded to me, 'Off you go then.' The wall looked confusing and I had no idea what to do with my hands or feet. *How hard can it be?* I thought. I stepped up to the wall, and placed my hands on the chalky, resin holds.

My fingers instinctively gripped as tightly as they could. I stepped off the ground and felt my weight pulling me backwards. *Get to the top,* I told myself. *Remember to breathe.* I was wobbly on my legs, and bashed my feet into the wall as I stepped up each time, but the simplicity of reaching higher, pushing up with my legs, using my core to balance and tension as I stretched out for the next hold felt instinctive too. Primal. I looked through my feet and felt the rush every climber feels the first time they are 10 metres off the ground and clinging on by their fingertips – the exposure, the thrill. I loved it. I *knew* I was going to.

A few months later, on a blustery December afternoon at the end of 2008, I found myself clinging to a sea cliff on the south coast, as waves crashed beneath me like frothing concrete. Sea spray was attacking my eyes, but I couldn't release my grip to wipe away the salt. 'What now?' I shouted anxiously down to my climbing partner, my panicked voice betraying how scared I was.

'Just get your foot up, and you're at the top.'

'I can't.' My voice nearly cracked as I shouted back. I felt that if I moved an inch, I would lose my balance, and be spat off the rock and into the ferocious swell below.

'Just do it ...' my belayer shouted back. It was 3 p.m. and the sun was low in the sky. I had to get moving.

I looked all around me. My white fingers were clinging to cold rock. The wind blew my hair across my face. I didn't have much choice but to make the last move. I couldn't climb down, and I definitely didn't want to fall.

I would either land in the ocean and probably get smashed on to the rocks by the waves, or land next to my belayer on the ledge.

I shifted my balance to my right foot and scraped my left foot up the rock as high as I dared, pushing my tiptoes down on what looked like a big enough edge to be a foothold. I rocked my balance on to my left leg, and pushed my body weight down through the pressure point on my big toe, praying that my foot wouldn't slip as I stood up on it, and simultaneously released my left hand and slapped for the top of the cliff where, *thank god*, there was a huge 'jug' to grab. I pulled myself up over the cliff edge, the crashing waves disappeared, and the world became instantly calmer. In a second, I had gone from being gripped by fear to a rush of relief and pure joy.

It was my first outdoor 'lead' climb. My first milestone reached. I had come a long way since that first taster session at Craggy Island. I was one small step closer to Mount Everest.

I looked out towards the sea and the bays and cliffs in the distance. I breathed the cold December air into my lungs. I didn't want to be anywhere else. Everest had given me so much already. I was so thankful to that mountain, thousands of miles away, for introducing me to the world on my doorstep.

I had been lucky that, since that first indoor climb, I had got my foot in the door of a whole new world. The climbing community had opened up to me, and I had made new friends, who taught me, encouraged me, and showed me the wonderful climbing areas we had on our doorstep.

I had also become Everest's biggest super-fan. I devoured

every blog post, every book, every piece of information I could get my hands on about the mountain and the history of its expeditions. The more I read, the more I could visualise the climb and what it would be like. I would fall asleep each night dreaming of toiling my way up its slopes, risking my life for a chance on the summit. And every visit to the climbing wall was a chance to get myself one step closer to the brilliant stories I'd read about and endlessly played over in my mind.

December gave way to 1 January 2009. I woke up, invigorated by the clean slate of a new year and the possibilities it might bring. I pulled on my old running shoes and headed out through the door to begin one of my regular routes – a 9-mile loop around Windsor Great Park. It was below freezing, but I still wore my shorts and a vest top. No hat, no gloves. I told myself that this was it – I was training for Everest. Families wrapped up in long coats and scarves for their New Year's Day walk gawped as I ran past, my skin flushed red, my freezing breath clouding around me. I giggled at how silly I looked.

As the freezing winter gave way to the first colours of spring, the great Chomolungma was causing my life to change entirely. I needed money for climbing shoes and petrol, so I stopped going to Primark and buying Domino's and found a job as an assistant to a local guy, Luke, who needed extra help around his house. We became good friends, and eventually Luke inspired me to support a disability charity in conjunction with my Mount Everest attempt. I spent my first pay cheque at Snow and Rock in Chertsey on climbing shoes and a harness. I was so proud of those pieces of kit; I knew that they were the key to some amazing experiences in the future.

As I gained confidence, proud of my progress, I jumped on the blogging bandwagon, where I regaled probably zero people with stories of my climbing excursions and long-distance 'training' runs: 'The heaving lungs, dizzy head (I was so hot, I got badly dehydrated and sunburnt) and burning legs led to a fatigue that I have never experienced before but – even though I was nearly fainting from the dehydration, my legs screaming in pain – I was still running! It was a euphoric moment.'

Sometimes it would be easy to trust those moments of euphoria, that sense of knowing that somehow, everything was going to be OK. In those moments, the whole world felt right. It felt as though I was always born to be in the mountains, but was only just discovering the fact. It sounds silly, but I often thought about 'destiny' and told myself that I was following mine.

However, like everyone on an uncertain path, these moments would be met equally with self-doubt. I would find myself looking at my situation in a different light. Logic would tell me that my real chances of ever making it to Everest were almost impossible. Even Kenton had said that 99 per cent of people who said they wanted to climb Everest never did. I found myself asking: *What makes you think you're that special? Whenever have you been extraordinary?*

Sometimes, that reasonable voice of logic would become more irrational and fatalistic. I would wake up convinced that I would never be strong enough to climb in the death zone, that I was a fake, and really I didn't deserve to be there. I would have days when my mind-set was that of my anxious teenage self again: *What if you fail? This is a waste of time. People like you don't climb mountains like Everest.* I would have a bad run, and tell myself I wasn't an athlete and would never be fit enough. I would go climbing with my friends and have a near panic attack at a really crucial moment on a climb, and become convinced that I wasn't cut out to be a mountaineer.

When I look back, I can see that I was dealing with so much uncertainty and was so alone in my challenge, that I couldn't tell if I was on the right track or not. I often felt like the only person in the world who understood what I was going through.

When I was frustrated, I reminded myself that it wasn't all about the end point. Climbing just for the sake of climbing made me happy. If Everest did come to nothing, as the devil on my shoulder would tell me, I would tell it that I didn't care. Climbing was enough.

I reminded myself that while my situation was far away from Everest, I knew that my attitude was in the right place. It's hard to beat someone if they never give up. When an opportunity came up, I always grasped it. When I had a bad day, I tried to learn why and not make the same mistakes next time. I have always been one of those people that like to keep doing something until I get it right.

The self-doubt was even motivating at times. The voices in my head kept me on my toes. I wouldn't allow myself to miss a run, or not make the last move of a difficult climb; because if I did, I was only feeding the uncertainty. I was trying to escape from my worst fears – that actually, people like me couldn't climb mountains like Everest. I clung to the hope and belief that if I gave it everything I had, my hard work would pay off.

I told myself to trust that feeling. That if I kept taking those small steps, eventually an opportunity would arise. I just had to keep getting out there, and climbing as much as possible until I found the answers I was looking for. I didn't know how long this process would take me to work out, but I knew for sure that I would never climb Mount Everest if I sat at home in my bedroom looking at cat videos on YouTube.

After that first outdoor lead climb I was lucky enough to go on many adventures, from looking down on a cloud inversion from the summit of Snowdon in North Wales, to wading through the knee-deep snow of Coire an t-Sneachda in the breathtaking mountains of the Scottish Cairngorms. Every weekend was a new experience, and a new discovery – whether it was about myself, or the world around me. My eyes and my heart had been thrown wide open.

After spending the winter learning to climb in the UK, spring arrived in the Alps and in June I flew to Chamonix to climb with a Mountain Guide who was a friend of Kenton's. We scaled Gran Paradiso, a 4,061-metre peak in Italy, and attempted Mont Blanc, which at 4,810 metres is the highest mountain in western Europe. Unfortunately the weather thwarted our attempt, with 60 km/h gusts threatening to blow us off our feet. Even in the tough conditions and the biting altitude, I still felt strong. Altitude is such an unknown, and I remember thinking, *yes – my body does adapt!* It felt like another sign in some ways. I was good at altitude and that meant I was born to climb mountains. I also loved being on bigger peaks for the first time – the long days, early starts, huge exposure – being up above. I realised that every moment I spent in the mountains was a moment I didn't want to spend anywhere else.

Despite failing to climb Mont Blanc, Kenton was pleased to hear about my progress. It might sound crazy, but after that week in the Alps he decided that I was experienced enough that autumn to attempt my first 8,000-metre peak. He called me up, and invited me to climb Mount Manaslu.

Mount Manaslu, 8,156 metres, stands in the Nepalese Himalayas. On the phone, Kenton had described the peak as a beautiful spire, surrounded by glaciers that poured down from its summit slopes like lava. The climbing would involve everything from crossing crevasse fields to steep pitches of blue ice with avalanche-prone territory around. Above 7,000 metres, they planned to use bottled oxygen.

I listened to Kenton describe the climb to me on the phone and my spirit soared and then sank before he had finished speaking. I would have given *anything* to be on that expedition. But it was too soon. I needed more time. I asked Kenton if he thought I was ready for such a big leap, and he said 'Bonita, don't go expecting it to be easy, because it won't be. It will be really, really tough. Go with the attitude that it doesn't matter if you don't reach the summit, because being on that mountain will teach you so much. You won't regret it.'

I knew he was right. Sometimes you just have to go for things, even when they come round sooner than expected. It was a huge step that in an ideal world I wouldn't have taken so soon, but life doesn't always follow best-laid plans. As the saying goes, 'Be stubborn about your goals but flexible about your methods.' An opportunity had come up, and I would have to find a way to be able to grasp it and make the most I could from it.

I reasoned with myself that the only way I would ever find out whether I was good enough to attempt Mount Manaslu was by going and attempting it. For better or for worse, at least I would have some concrete answers to work with.

I signed up, and told myself there was no pressure. I was going on the expedition to learn as much as I could about what it was like to climb and survive in the Himalayas. Nothing more. The thought of ever reaching the summit was beyond me. But just going to see what it was like lower down on the mountain, that I could do.

Finally, I had something concrete that I could train for, and a response for people when they asked me, 'So when are you actually going to climb a mountain?' Whenever I thought about Mount Manaslu, I felt shit-scared and then excited in equal measure. I knew that a life-changing adventure sat just a few months away, an adventure that a year ago I could never have dreamed I would embark on. With every day that passed on the countdown to the departure date of 28 August 2009, I felt sick to my stomach with worry and uncertainty as to whether I would be fit and ready, but also wanted to burst with excitement. Manaslu meant another step towards Everest, and it meant escaping from university and life in Egham once and for all.

In those final few months of university, I was always at the climbing wall, on a weekend trip or on a long training run. I managed a 2:1. When I started my degree I had been unsure whether Media Arts was actually what I wanted to do. I had decided to go anyway, hoping that uni would at least broaden my horizons and introduce me to more opportunities than if I stayed in Wokingham and got a job. When I handed in my last piece of work, I knew I had made the right decision by not overthinking it. I felt thankful, not because I had fallen in love with my degree, but because my degree had introduced me to my love of the mountains. Sometimes you just have to do things even when you're not sure about them. I went to uni promising myself that an education was a huge blessing, and that if I kept an open mind, it would be worth it. I could never have imagined just how much that promise to myself was right.

Royal Holloway supported my crazy dream too, by sponsoring my place on the Manaslu expedition through their Annual Fund. To them, it didn't matter that I wasn't pursuing something to do with my degree, it was about supporting me as an individual whose most formative years had been spent within the Royal Holloway family.

When summertime came my friends and I went and slept in a cave along the Dorset coastline, falling asleep to the sounds of waves crashing into the cliffs below. I remember looking out one night from my sleeping bag and staring up at the stars. The midnight breeze rustled my hair. Everest was out there. Something told me that one day I would look at the stars from that mountain. I was on the right path. I just had to do my best on Manaslu.

Finally, the day before our departure date came. Our student house was packed up, my room stripped of the Everest books that had filled my shelves and the prayer flags that I'd hung above my bed. Photos of nights out with friends, littered with pictures of me out on climbing trips, smiling from beneath a helmet, often with chalk smeared across my face, were taken down off the walls and everything was put into bags. For now, my home would be transient. I would be moving back to my mum's in September, but for the next five weeks I would be travelling through Nepal, each night sleeping higher and higher, until hopefully we would be camping at one of the highest places on Earth – Camp Four at 7,200 metres.

I took one last look at my room, knowing that I would never see it again, but also feeling as if so much of me had grown and developed within those four walls. I had spent so many nights staring at the ceiling dreaming of mountains. The era of dreaming was over. Now, it was time to go and live out the dreams.

That afternoon I went for a bike ride with Luke. My senses were so heightened – to the sweet smell of the grass, the glorious views across farmland and Windsor Great Park; to the beautiful blue sky and the sun warming my shoulders. I knew I wouldn't see another summer's day again for a long time. I drank in the moment. Soon, it would feel a world away.

The next day, 28 August, I stepped on to the plane at Gatwick Airport. As the plane took off and home disappeared beneath the clouds, I realised that it had been less than a year ago that I'd sat in that lecture which had changed everything. *What if I hadn't gone that night? What if I had stayed at home and watched TV?*

There are so many 'sliding doors' moments in life – opportunities that we have missed without even being aware we have done so. Seeing how easily I could have missed discovering this passion for climbing taught me the importance of always keeping an open mind. It taught me to try and say yes more, not to pigeon-hole myself into thinking I can or can't do certain things. To remember that I am always capable of morphing and changing into a person I never imagined possible.

I thanked my lucky stars that on the night of that lecture, I hadn't questioned my reasons for going too much; I hadn't talked myself out of it before I'd even arrived. I had asked myself 'What's the worst that can happen?' As we cruised towards Nepal at 30,000 feet, I wondered what the final answer to that question would be. Would my worst fears be confirmed or my wildest dreams fulfilled? I was about to find out.

CHAPTER 6

On 29 August 2009 I arrived in Kathmandu, the capital of
Nepal and the gateway for many 8,000-metre peak expeditions, including my own. The air was heavy with smog
and the sickly smell of incense. The din of thousands of
mopeds was ever present.

I felt like a giant, towering head and shoulders above the
locals who milled around me. My blonde hair made me
even more conspicuous. I wandered out of the dark-
panelled airport into the hustle of an early Kathmandu
evening. There, waiting for me, was a great giant of a man
in a linen shirt with a prayer scarf around his neck. 'You
must be Bonita.' He looked me up and down. 'OK, fine.
You're a good size.'

I guessed he was referring to my puppy fat.

That was my first encounter with Henry Todd, otherwise
known as the Todd Father. Henry organises expeditions,
and has been taking teams out to the Himalayas for over
thirty years. Henry is as sharp as a knife and fiercely opin-
ionated. He was to become pivotal in my development as
a climber. He was the man who pushed me and what I
thought I was capable of to the limit, the man who would
see me through my proudest achievements and would become a good friend.

'Your chopper probably won't fly tomorrow,' he says.

'Two just crashed into each other so it's a bit of a hoo-ha.'

'Are you not flying with us?'

'No. Some of us are walking. We always walk. It's much better for the body.'

I instantly knew that I wanted to do the trek instead of going by helicopter. When I had read the plans for the expedition, I had been disappointed to see that we were getting a helicopter from Kathmandu to just below Manaslu Base Camp and I couldn't understand why. I wanted to experience the journey through Nepal as much as the mountain itself, but if that's what the team were doing, I wasn't going to leave them. Now I knew that some of them felt the same way, and I knew which group I wanted to join. I asked Henry.

'OK, fine,' he said. 'It's not going to be nice: leeches, floods, landslides, bed bugs, the heat ...'

It was exactly the adventure I'd been dreaming about.

The next day, the trekking group of Henry and myself, and two others – Dave and Emma – took a ten-hour jeep ride from Kathmandu into the Manaslu region. I had been violently sick out of the side of the jeep and found a puncture hole on my leg where a leech had had its fill.

When our truck broke down from the unrelenting crashes into mud banks and obscured boulders, we had to stop and ask some friendly locals to help fix it. With no idea about mechanics, I stood with the commotion behind me and watched the sun set over the luscious paddy fields. The flowing shapes of the terraces reflected the evening light and glimmered gold and silver in amongst pockets of vibrant green. It was peaceful and magical.

I awoke the next morning to the growling barks of a

dog, and the gentle hustle and bustle of the street outside. I sat up and looked out of the window with bleary morning eyes – ramshackle wooden buildings lined a dirt-track street that was bustling with women in bright saris and kids in crisp white school uniforms. Beyond the row of dwellings was wild jungle, almost creeping up and swallowing the village whole.

This village (called Aright) was the final frontier – there were no roads left for the jeep to drive on. We would be looking to find shelter each night in the homes of farmers along the way. I was both excited and scared of what lay ahead.

That day we walked through endless paddy fields that were tended to by the hands of petite women in brightly coloured saris. Then, through beautiful valleys, with water-falls thundering down all around us. As the paddy fields gave way to the steeper terrain, we trekked through dense jungle and forest; other times crumbling paths took us high up above the river and gave us a chance to see the snowy Himalayan peaks in the distance.

At night we stayed in mostly wooden tea-houses or people's homes, and would be in bed just after sunset. Toilets were holes in the ground and the food was the same every day: rice, boiled potatoes, chapattis, and dahl.

As we approached the Tibetan border, the land became wilder. Gone were the bright-green rice fields cut like steps into the foothills. The river, which was wide and flat, had now become more treacherous as we climbed higher.

We found that the people looked and dressed differently too. The women we had seen tending to paddy fields at lower altitudes wore delicate saris; the women here dressed in heavy woollen tunics with leather belts adorned with silver trinkets. They looked hardened, weathered by the harshness of a life spent living in the mountains.

After one miserable morning walking through mud and rain, I finally reached the village where we planned to stop for lunch. I stepped over the threshold into the dark and smoke to find an open fire burning in the middle of the single-room hut, a Nepalese woman sitting cross-legged on the floor and straining tea over the stove. Emma and Henry were already sitting with her, tucking into a tin of pâté and crackers for lunch.

I sat down on the creaking floorboards and, trying not to choke on the smoke, smiled at the lady. She gave me a toothless smile back, her icy-blue eyes lighting up the dark room. There wasn't anywhere in the world I would rather be.

Some nights there wouldn't be a tea-house for trekkers to stay in, so we would ask a local if we could stay in their home. We would sit with their children on the floor and share a bowl of boiled potatoes for dinner, each taking our turn to dip them into yak butter and salt. The toddlers all had beautiful dark eyes and chubby red cheeks, their faces muddy from play. I'll never forget their smiles and laughter. And the kindness of strangers. I remember thinking that, in the UK, people have everything and yet give very little away. Here in Nepal, people had very little but would share with you everything they had. *Maybe happiness is nothing to do with wealth?* This was the first time I had really thought about that.

One night, as we lay in bed in the house of a man who had agreed to shelter us for the evening, I stared up at the corrugated-iron roof – it was full of gaps and holes and I could see the stars. I thought about all those nights that I had stared at my ceiling in my room at university; how trapped I had felt and how I had longed to go on the adventures I'd read about in books. Now, here I was. I felt so grateful that I had the opportunity to make those dreams a reality. Later, a thunderstorm poured down, and raindrops splattered through the holes in the roof. I got soaked, and the raindrops hitting my face kept me awake all night.

The next day we stopped in a village that had a phone and we were asked if we wanted to use it. At first I felt uneasy about contacting the outside world. I felt so at home trekking through the mountains that I didn't want to face the fact that I was someone else to those I'd left behind. At home, I was 'Bonnie the clumsy clot' as my mum would call me, and well known amongst my friends for being scatty and 'all over the place' when it came to being organised. Out here in the Himalayas, this trek had given me the chance to start re-writing who I was and who I wanted to become, but this new 'me' was fragile and in its infacy. To call home would shatter the delicate new skin I'd started building for myself.

Eventually, I decided I would call my mum, as I knew how much she would be worried about me, and I needed to stop being so precious and think of others too. As the phone began to ring, I felt tears rise in my chest. It was a shock to feel that emotion. No answer. Somehow, even without speaking to my mum, those few seconds holding the phone to my ear brought back all my memories of home. It was as if I'd left them at the edge of the jungle and, for a second, they had caught up with me.

On the final day, as we walked up a steep rocky path to

Manaslu Base Camp, which sat at 4,800 metres, the amphi-theatre of jagged spires surrounded me. The mountains were my audience, willing me on. We walked up through a deep fog and lashings of rain. I couldn't see my teammates in front of me. The air felt thin and I struggled to gasp enough oxygen into my lungs. This was the highest I'd ever been.

As I slipped back downwards on some scree, a voice said, 'If you're finding it hard now, you won't stand a chance later on.' *No!* I thought. *I'm not listening to you.* For some reason, I'd had a song in my head since the day before: 'Something Inside So Strong' by Labi Siffre. I felt as though the mountains were singing the words to me. As my foot slipped again and I fell on to my hands, I had those lyrics in my head.

I knew as things got harder, I was going to have to fight harder, to find strength within myself that I didn't know existed. I remembered my stepdad's words to me as a little girl: 'This is when you choose whether to become a good runner or a very good runner ...' I had to become some-thing new, and I was. I could feel it happening with every step.

I struggled to catch my breath as I staggered up the final few metres of scree. The mountain beckoned us, single file, into its grasp.

I could now see the reds and oranges of our tents dotted across the moonscape in the distance, appearing and disappearing in the flurries of wind. I heard the first deep rumble from inside the mountain. It was a sinister sound, and I instantly feared it.

The fog engulfed us, cutting off the world below our

feet. The paddy fields and luscious jungle were gone. We were now in a land of rock and ice.

Base Camp finally came into view, and the smiling faces of our support team came out of the fog to greet us. They were Nepalese Sherpas, who had been employed by Henry Todd on his expeditions for many years. The warmth from their toothy smiles and cups of tea pressed into our cold and shivering hands was exactly what I needed. Bhim, the team cook, gave me a hug, and I felt relieved that, for now, this was home. We laughed, we cried. We had made it. It was 7 September, only a week into the expedition, but already I felt like I'd come so far.

I threw my bags down in front of the nearest tent, collapsed inside and closed my eyes. My heart fluttered in my chest, trying to compensate for the lack of oxygen – now there was now only 50 per cent of it available with each breath compared to sea level.

As my breathing settled, the roar of distant avalanches sharpened my senses. I lay there and listened to the crashing and cracking and felt the ground rumbling. It sounded like a mystical beast trying to fight its way out of the innards of the mountain. This was a new world compared to the one I'd spent the last week immersed in.

I relived the past week in my head. Eating potatoes with those toddlers by an open fire, laughing with Emma as we ran from monkeys throwing rocks and sticks at us, taking a moment to breathe in the frigid air rising from the mountain river, having a shower in a waterfall. I knew I would cherish these memories for the rest of my life.

The trek was another 'sliding doors' moment that I could

so easily never have experienced. I could have simply got a 45-minute chopper ride. My quest to climb Everest had shown me once again how keeping an open mind, not always taking the easy or expected option, could lead us to the most wonderful adventures in life.

I fell asleep to the chorus of avalanches crashing down all around us, feeling humbled that my legs, my mind and my beating heart had got me this far. I could only hope that I could keep up with my team, now that the real climbing was about to start.

CHAPTER 7

When you hear the sound of an avalanche up close, it feels as if the world is about to end.

The deafening roar of thousands of tonnes of ice crashing downwards surrounds you and vibrates in your bones. In a split second, fear grips you in a vice and you are paralysed by the realisation that there's nothing you can do. *This is it.* You are about to die. But that's not as bad as what follows a half-second later: regret. The worst regret you could imagine. The moment when you realise that your life is over, and you'll never get it back.

A second too long passes. *Surely I should be dead by now?* You start to orientate the sound – it's gone quiet. The roar whispers to a silence. Over just as it began. You're not going to die after all. *What am I doing here?* Nothing in the world seems more pointless than choosing to be somewhere where death teases you so grotesquely.

I lay awake that first night at Manaslu Base Camp listening to those avalanches and the cracking of the glacier underneath our sleeping bags. It was as if the mountain was threatening us ... warning us to leave. If Base Camp felt dangerous, what the hell lay ahead? Was it my instincts telling me to run, or was it just fear of the unknown?

I listened for noises from my teammates' tents. Emma's

tent was next to mine. Was she scared too? Somehow I thought not. They were all experienced mountaineers and I felt out of my comfort zone just being in their company. *What was I doing here in their world? Why had I persuaded myself to do this?*

I longed for daylight to come. I longed for the month to pass quickly so that I would finally be able to go home. I wondered whether I would ever go home. *Maybe this is the last place I'll ever know?*

For the next four weeks, I spent pretty much every waking moment trying to cope with the panicked surges of fear and uncertainty. My heart, already struggling from the altitude at 4,800 metres, was also having to calm the sudden floods of adrenaline, constant cortisol and the heartache of homesickness.

Everything was new to me, and I had no idea how I would cope with the challenges that lay ahead. I had no reference point, no idea at all of whether I would die of altitude sickness, or the below-freezing temperatures, or fall to my death.

All I had to console myself in my darkest moments was the promise that I would take things one step at a time. That if right now, I was OK, then that was all that mattered. I was also lucky to have the support of my team, and their words of encouragement that I would be OK.

I had not slept at all the night before we stepped on to the hill for the first time. We had set our alarms for 5 a.m. and, when mine buzzed, I was still awake. The dread that filled my stomach is hard to describe. I would rather have been anywhere in the world in that moment than about to face the Manaslu glacier for the first time. I wanted to curl up in my sleeping bag and disappear.

I heard Emma's voice outside my tent. 'You OK, Bon?'

'Yeah,' I croaked back, wiping my teary eyes. I promised myself that if I didn't like it today, I would just pack my bags and head home. *Come on. You can do this*, I told myself.

Emma was only a few years older than me, in her late twenties. She was tall and had long blonde hair and the kind of attitude that I could tell had been built out of years of working and living as a trekking guide. Nothing fazed her – not the discomfort of cramped tent conditions, or being faced with near-death moments. She always saw the funny side in a situation, no matter how bad it was. Emma showed me how your attitude to a situation can change everything – not just for you, but for your whole team. Emma's positivity and laughter often stopped me from feeling so sorry for myself, and on that first day of climbing the mountain, I knew that if I stuck with her, maybe her energy would carry me through.

I climbed out of the tent and said good morning to her. She was, as usual, full of energy and cracking jokes. Within moments I was laughing with her and saw the vapour of my breath crystallise in the air. Looking up, I saw that we were under a blanket of stars. For just a second, things weren't so bad.

Rob Casserley was there too, sat on a rock stuffing dry sacks full of food and a stove and gas into his rucksack, his matted blond hair poking out from his striped blue hat and layers of red and orange string hung from his neck – gifts from Buddhist monks from his many expeditions to

Nepal. He had trekked in two days behind us and despite a stomach bug, was determined to join us for the first day on the hill.

As we climbed across the Manaslu glacier that first day, my teammates and I were no more than tiny little ants in this world of giants, insignificant flecks on a mighty landscape, at the mercy of mother nature. Avalanches rocketed down all around us as we nervously negotiated crevasse after crevasse, often jumping backwards in horror as weak snow collapsed beneath our feet, exposing drops over 100 metres deep.

I was incredibly impressed by how resilient both Emma and Rob were as we weaved our way in and out of this deadly maze. I watched their fierce focus on the moment in front of them. *Perhaps the key to climbing the highest mountains in the world is just to get on with it?* I thought. To *not* think too much.

That night, I borrowed Rob's satellite phone and called my dad. As I spoke to him, I realised again that the most brilliant stars were lighting up the night sky. 'I wish you could see this, Dad.' In that moment, I felt lucky again.

The next day, climbing through thick snowfall on a rope with Henry Todd, a gaping hole opened up beneath my feet and I started falling, the walls of a crevasse rushing past me, my stomach suspended for a moment as I went into free fall. Just as I thought, *This is it*, the rope jolted violently and I came to an abrupt halt. Henry had stopped my fall. He had thrown himself backwards into the snow and dug his feet into the ground as my weight shock loaded the rope and yanked violently at his harness, snapping into his back.

'You're OK, Bonita,' he shouted. 'Don't cry!'

As I dangled there in the beautiful black glistening ice of the crevasse, I didn't know which was worse. The horror of thinking I was falling to my death, or the realisation that I was the team's cry-baby.

I learnt a lot about myself and a lot about teamwork in those hours I was physically tied to Henry, Emma, Rob or Dave. I learnt that, however bad I was feeling, I had their lives in my hands with every step I took. For me to allow myself to lose my concentration, to get upset and emotional, was to put everyone else at risk. For the sake of my team, I had to toughen up. I had to stay sharp and quell the voices in my head. Whether I liked it or not, I had to put them first. They had entrusted their lives to me by tying into the same rope. I knew how much respect that demanded. And when I tied into that rope every morning, I reminded myself of that. Over time, it got easier to deal with my demons at night, and put them aside during the day. I was proud of our team when we reached a new high point, or climbed really well together.

Most nights, I lay awake gripped by the noises of the mountain. I would be desperate for sleep to come, knowing how exhausted I'd be the next day on that rope, my team-mates shouting for me to keep pace on the dangerous glacier. Equally, I was so scared about what the next day might bring, I was scared to go to sleep. Up in the high camps, I would hear my teammates snoring next to me while I would lie wide awake, my cheeks stained with tears. I longed so much for a proper bed, a safe bed where avalanches couldn't bury me. The longing was so deep, it physically hurt.

With each new day, I awoke with a pit in my stomach, wondering how on earth I was going to get through it. If it was anything like the day before, I would question whether I could go on any longer.

In mid September, halfway through the expedition, climbing across avalanched slopes on fixed lines, I looked up and saw some of my teammates far up ahead of me, almost like a mirage in the distance. Rob was kindly waiting behind me, making sure I was OK. I knew I had hours left of climbing in the heat. My water bottle had run out hours before. I was sweating through my clothes, and gasping constantly for air. The altitude was stripping me of everything I had. *This is the hardest day of my life*, I thought to myself. *I know it is.* I had never felt so emotionally and physically drained before.

That, in a way, was a great moment as much as it was an awful one. I felt a rare sense of pride in knowing and being able to pinpoint the hardest day of my life. Nothing I had ever done, from overcoming my eating disorder to my hardest training climbs could come close to the willpower and energy I was needing to summon that day. The pride gave way to the overwhelming feeling of helplessness. *Please let it be over*, I begged – to myself, and to the mountain. Blue ice glimmered in the distance. The wall cascaded towards me in waves – ledges and bulges and swooping sections of blank, bulletproof ice called *sastrugi*.

You can't do this, the voice said in my mind. I could feel the familiar switch starting to turn. My irrational demons were raising their ugly heads. *It's impossible. You're never going to make it. You don't care about this mountain and you don't care about Everest. Just go home.*

My screaming legs, my gasping lungs, my clouded mind – everything was screaming at me to stop. 'I can't do it,' I said aloud. Rob was by my side. 'Yes, you can,' he said. 'Trust me, when you most want to give up, you have got so much more to give. I've been there. I know how you feel. Just take one more step.'

Somehow, Rob always said the right thing.

I was thinking of turning around and walking down the mountain, so what was stopping me from walking upwards? I didn't physically have to give up. It must, therefore, have been mental. Rob had given me a moment of clarity in the most crucial of moments. He stopped the demons from winning that time. If I can take a step downwards, I can take one upwards. This isn't physical, it's mental. What's stopping me is my imagination. I'm terrified of what lies ahead, convinced that everything that can kill me, will. *Maybe,* I thought, *I just have to stop thinking and start doing. Maybe if I can just focus on that very next step, and not look up at the climb ahead, that wouldn't scare me so much, and maybe I would be able to take one more step.*

One more step, I said to myself, *and then you can go home if you want.* I took the step and absolutely nothing happened. So I said to myself again, *Take one more step, and then you can go home.*

After a long day, just focusing on one step at a time, I collapsed into camp. I'd done it. When I looked back down at the head wall, I couldn't believe it – it had passed by in a blur.

That day was the biggest breakthrough in my climbing career, because it taught me that the biggest mountains are just in our minds. Our imaginations have this incredible ability to freak us out and tell us we can't do things. The reality, I realised, was so very different – I was far more capable than I thought I was.

From that day onwards, it went from the worst of times to the best of times. We climbed higher and higher up Mount Manaslu, emerging from the shadows of the mountain and into what felt like another atmosphere. We got the rewards for all our suffering: the most incredible views.

Oceans of cloud stretched out beneath us. I looked out at the Himalayas at my feet and felt so grateful to that girl who took that one step up the mountain a week ago, instead of going down. If I had gone down that day, I would never have seen all this. The sunrises and sunsets, for instance, I won't forget until my last breath. I am so glad I didn't give up when I most wanted to.

The rest of the climb wasn't plain sailing. I went to sleep most nights, crammed into a tent with two or three others, feeling my aching body sink once more into the cold, hard ice. I would look back on each day and think, *That was the hardest day of my life.* The next day, I would go to bed thinking, *No, that wasn't the hardest day of my life, this one was.* Every day we climbed higher, the more broken and exhausted I would become. I had no idea where I was getting my reserves from. But I also noticed, broken as I was, that I was finding my rhythm. As each day passed, I managed to stay a little closer to my team. Lots of people slowed down, but I found myself speeding up. It wasn't that I was getting stronger – it was that my body and mind were learning new boundaries, new ways of being. What once felt impossible was now my everyday routine. I couldn't believe how quickly I could adjust.

On 25 September 2009, we were headed for the summit. After what felt like an age, I started to notice out of my peripheral vision that I was no longer surrounded by darkness. The sky was now a mix of baby blue and grey, tinged with pink and yellow. The peaks that I had once craned my neck to look up at were now miles below me. They looked so small and distant. The summits were lit orange against the grey sky, burning bright like candle flames. A new day holding so much promise.

Sunrise happens every day and has done for millennia, and yet, on that day, I was there to see it, not just staring up from below, but with the best view on Earth. I was looking down at our planet, watching the Earth come to life, wakening from its slumber for miles around me. *How lucky, how unbelievably lucky am I to see this?*

The false summit soon came into sight. We had decided as a team not to climb to the true summit – it's only another 10 metres higher, but there were no fixed ropes there and we agreed it was too dangerous to climb without rope, and too dangerous to hang around in the dead zone waiting for it, using up precious oxygen. The end of this exhausting, miserable, thrilling, life-changing expedition was near. It was so close I could almost touch it.

It took one last lung-busting pull up over the lip of the final wall of ice and snow. The usual thoughts were flashing through my mind: *I can't do this*. But by this point, I was so exhausted, I couldn't even pay attention to them.

Just do it. Stop thinking. So I did. I felt the pain, I let the searing heat of lactic burn flood through me; I let the gasping heaves of my breath scramble for attention without trying to control them. I let the sweat drip down my back and the grip of my hands ache. It was the last few steps; soon, it would be over, for a few minutes at least.

I could see the sun shining brightly above me. I kicked those last few steps, and there I was, a pile in the snow, lying on the false summit of Mount Manaslu, the eighth-highest mountain in the world. I was twenty-one years old, and I had just become one of the youngest people ever to climb to this height on the peak.

I looked out around me and in all directions I could see the curvature of the Earth on the horizon. The one thing that had inspired me so much in the beginning. When I looked out and saw the blueish hue, I had a deep sense of knowing – it was like I could feel it in my bones, I knew I could climb Everest now – it was only a few hundred metres higher than Manaslu – with the right support and with enough training, I knew I could do it.

We huddled on the summit for a few minutes before starting our descent. It had been the most life-changing experience in so many ways, and now all of a sudden – it was time to go home. We stepped off the summit, and started our two-day descent back to the safety of Base Camp.

As I packed up my things at Base Camp, with one mountain behind me, another one loomed closely in my mind. It wasn't a physical mountain, but the obvious impossibility of getting to Everest itself. My Manaslu expedition had cost a few thousand pounds, which was kindly paid for by my university, my savings, and a bit of cash from my dad. To climb Everest with Kenton, on the other hand, was going to cost a near-impossible $50,000.

I knew that there were cheaper operators on Everest, but I also knew that with my limited experience, I needed to climb the mountain with someone who I could trust in an emergency situation. Kenton had climbed Everest seven times and was widely known as one of the best guides on the mountain. When I first stated my interest in Kenton's Everest trips, he told me that Rob Casserley would be one of our team, and I wanted to climb with him just as much as I did with Kenton. Whilst $50,000 sounded like a lot of money, it seemed like I would be climbing with the two best mountaineers possible. However, there was the one small problem that I didn't have $50,000 in my back pocket. And I couldn't see how I would ever get that kind of money together in my entire life.

Still, I was fresh off my first 8,000-metre peak, I didn't have a job (except working part time for Luke) and I was in possibly the best situation I was ever going to be in my entire life to dedicate time and energy to making this crazy dream of climbing Everest a reality. The next Everest season was fast approaching – in the spring of 2010. There are two seasons on Everest every year, one which takes place pre-monsoon in the spring, and the other takes place post-monsoon in the autumn. Realistically, climbing in the monsoon or in the winter is incredibly dangerous and very few people have ever attempted such a feat. I wanted to be on Kenton's spring 2010 Everest expedition, and that meant I had six months before his intended departure date from the UK on the 1 April. Six months to find $50,000 and get ready for the biggest challenge of my life.

How was I going to find that kind of cash? My one option, I figured, having seen other mountaineers do it in the past, was to find a company to sponsor my place on Kenton's team. I would create a sponsorship brochure and cold call companies until one of them agreed to work with me, whether it was a hundred phone calls or a thousand. I figured that if I left no stone unturned, and made enough phone calls, eventually I would find the right company. All I knew was that they were never going to knock on my door. I had to go out and find them.

CHAPTER 8

*'Commitment is doing the thing you said you'd do, long
after you said you'd do it.'*

It's fair to say that if you announce one day out of the
blue that you are going to climb Mount Everest, your family
will not necessarily take you too seriously.

Back in the comforts of my mum's house after the adventure on Mount Manaslu, I finally sat them down and told
them what my true plan was. I didn't just announce it over
a cup of tea. I created a PowerPoint presentation about
Everest and my action plan of how I was going to climb
it.

I even invited my dad over to my mum's house to hear
my speech. One of the most surreal moments that Everest
gave me was looking at my dad sitting down on my mum's
sofa. It seemed the mountain's ability to effect change was
far-reaching in ways I couldn't have imagined.

I started my presentation, but I never got beyond the
first slide. My mum butted in immediately: 'People like us
don't climb mountains like Everest!'

My stepdad chimed in: 'Bonnie, you are so clumsy, you
will die if you try to do this.' He carried on, 'And I'm a
businessman, and I know that no company is going to

sponsor you in this recession. I'm sorry, darling. Get it out of your head. It's not going to happen.'

We argued on like that all evening. When I started to get emotional, my mum said, 'Why are you getting upset? We care about you, and as your parents we have to stop you from doing this. If you died, it would be our fault.'

I felt my voice – and the fire behind it that had kept me going since the start of this journey – shrink and die. They were right. I was deluded.

Then, my dad spoke up: 'I think this could be Bonnie's gold medal.'

My mum glared at my dad across the room, and that was it, the meeting was over, my slideshow unplayed, my dad ushered out of the living room, leaving behind a sour atmosphere. When I said goodbye to him at the front door he said, 'If this is your dream, you have to go for it.'

My dad, from day one, was always my biggest support. He was the only person who could see Everest as I saw it – the dream of a lifetime.

I shut the door behind him and walked past the living room, ignoring my parents, and rushed straight upstairs to run a bath. I sank into the water and felt tears rising in my chest. *That was a total disaster.* Everest couldn't have felt more impossible in that moment. I felt my frustration and anger slowly drain away, and by the time I was out of the bath I had made up my mind – I wanted to show my parents that people like us *could* climb mountains like Everest. I was going to prove them wrong.

That was the funny thing about my blind determination to climb that mountain – it didn't seem to matter what came my way, even when I had moments of thinking that all hope was lost, it still came back. The fire was never truly extinguished.

I woke up the next morning, resolved to prove my parents wrong, and turn those thoughts in my head into reality.

I carefully created a sponsorship brochure, where I'd agonised over every picture and word. Once it was ready, I decided that there was nothing left for it but to pick up the phone. With no contacts, no family connections and no idea of how to get in touch with the right people in an organisation, I thought I had nothing to lose but should just make that first call. As it rang, I prayed that nobody would answer. I didn't have a clue what I was going to say.

A chirpy woman answered the phone and, as the words started to come out of my mouth, the fear melted away. She kindly told me that she was not able to forward my call on to anyone in her company if I didn't have their name, and put the phone down. It was a total failure, but I'd also learnt an important piece of the puzzle – I needed names. With each phone call, I always learnt something new.

I would send out my sponsorship brochures with personalised covering letters, explaining to each company exactly why I believed they could benefit from sponsoring my expedition. I never heard back from a single one that I sent out. I learnt another lesson: that it was always best to try and speak to someone on the phone, or better, meet them in person.

During one rare meeting, I was walking into the boardroom of a financial services company and a door closed in my face, knocking the hot tea in my hand down my dress. Thankfully, the dress was black, but I sat through the meeting grimacing at the thought of the angry red burns I could feel underneath. Not surprisingly, the company didn't end up sponsoring the clumsy girl who spilt her tea.

Undeterred, I kept pushing for meetings, making phone calls and sending out my sponsorship brochure. In my eyes, every company was a potential partner. I would be in the car on the way back from a weekend climbing in Wales, and note down all the logos on the sides of lorries that rushed past.

Once, a friend of mine sent me the email address of his CEO. I promised him I wouldn't tell anyone at his company that he'd divulged such private information. When the CEO rang me moments after I sent the sponsorship brochure, I thought that I'd hit the jackpot. When he demanded to know where I'd got his email address from, I couldn't think fast enough on my feet and ended up putting the phone down on him.

The months passed on an endless merry-go-round of cold calls, emails, and meeting after wasted meeting. With every positive response, I would always get my hopes up and think 'This is it', only to be told once again that 'Sorry but we can't justify the cost in this recession.'

Christmas 2009 came, by which point I'd been on the sponsorship trail for nearly three months. I'd got nowhere, and time had flown by unreasonably fast. As the bleakest winter in living memory set in, everybody was complaining about the cold. I took the snow and freezing temperatures as a sign from above – they would be perfect training conditions. While my friends and family revelled in the usual Christmas excesses, I would be out on a late-night run, passing pubs filled to the brim with revellers. Sometimes I'd see my old Wokingham friends walking between bars on a Friday night as I ran through the centre of town. They'd just notice it was me as I ran past, them off to another cosy bar, me pounding the pavements for another hour, before going home and settling back down in front of my computer for another few hours of sending sponsorship emails.

I didn't feel jealous of my friends, and I didn't feel smug either. I just knew that if I wanted my dream to become a reality, I needed to have self-discipline. It was that simple.

Training wasn't just discipline, though, it was also time to escape. My time running was often the only respite I had from the toils of sponsorship hunting. It was the time when I felt momentarily closer to Everest. I told myself that all these hours pushing my physical and mental endurance would pay off the day I found myself in the death zone.

My night-time runs were brutal, my whole body fighting not to vomit during the last mile-long sprint uphill to my house. I would walk around the front garden afterwards to catch my breath and look up to see the lights on inside. I hoped that I wouldn't have yet another argument with my parents. I hated arguing with them. They wanted to hear a logical reason as to why I wanted to risk my life. I couldn't give them one. All I had was instinct.

I would turn the key in the front door, and within minutes another heated discussion would start.

'Who on Earth has money like that to spend in a recession when people are losing their jobs?' my stepdad tried to reason with me one night. I had no rebuttal, nothing I could present as a counter-argument, apart from the fact that I believed in the 1 per cent chance that Everest could happen. I was going to do everything I could to make sure that, if the chance came, I would grasp it. Again, in my stepdad Rob's eyes it was all a dangerous fantasy. A waste of time and a cruel thing for me to put them, my parents, through.

On Christmas Day 2009, I had almost every family member and friend take me to one side, glass of wine in one hand, mince pie in the other, and ask me, 'How could you put your mum through this?' It didn't seem to matter what answer I gave, it was never good enough. There is never a good enough reason to climb Everest – it is not altruistic, in fact it is incredibly selfish to risk your life for no discernible reason. I found myself asking the same questions of myself as I fell asleep each night. 'Am I really willing to risk my mother losing her daughter, just so that I can try and stand on top of the world?'

In truth, I couldn't find a good enough answer myself to that question. I just had a deep sense of intuition that everything would be OK. And I had to trust in that feeling, otherwise all justification was gone.

As the weather worsened, I took my training up a gear. I would load up my rucksack with books and do my old running route back to Royal Holloway University. Once it took me three hours as I slipped and slid the 16 miles over ice and snow, arriving at Egham train station to immediately get a train back to Wokingham, only to find that the rail network was at a standstill. I had no phone on me, so had no choice but to run to my dad's, a mere 9 miles away in Bracknell. By the time I made it to his, it was late at night and, after 25 miles in the cold, I was miserable. Dad would always drive me home, and on those drives, he would tell me to stick at it. 'Don't give up, Bons. The people who achieve in life are the ones who don't give up.'

At least I had training, or I did have, until one weekend in North Wales. Going berserk in the Glyders and on Snowdon, I was running full pelt down the Pyg Track and my foot slipped on some black ice, flying out in front of me. I landed in the splits. I'm not a gymnast, so the manoeuvre tore the adductor muscle in my left leg. I couldn't even lift my foot into the car once I'd hobbled back to the car park. Training resumed a few weeks later, but it was demoralising to see my body starting to fall apart as readily as my plans to find sponsorship.

Still, I was fit enough to run slowly, and would go out every Sunday with Auntie Belinda. We would run for three hours around the trails of Swinley Forest. Like my dad, she kept telling me to stick at it. The Norrises always told me to keep going. 'For how much longer?' I'd say back. 'I'm running out of time.'

My parents, seeing that months of criticism hadn't swayed me at all, eventually decided that if I was serious about Everest, then they would have to support me. My mum knew exactly how to help me – plenty of cups of tea – and just being able to bounce sponsorship ideas around with my stepdad made a huge difference.

Around this time, I met Tori James. She was the first Welsh woman to climb Mount Everest and held the record as the youngest British woman to climb the peak too. If I was successful on Everest, which was unlikely considering I didn't even have the ability to get to Base Camp at that point, then I would take her 'youngest British woman' record. I met Tori in a bar in London. She was wearing a sharp business suit, her red hair slicked back in a pony-tail – she had been speaking at a corporate event before she met me. She seemed so pulled together and success-ful – but so friendly and supportive when I told her my plans. She said to me, 'There wasn't a single day when I didn't do something towards Everest. Every day for years I did at least one thing – and that's what it takes, consist-ency, perseverance and discipline even when you most want to give in. Just keep doing something every day, and you'll get somewhere eventually.' I felt so pleased to hear that Tori had gone through a similar journey – she too had to find sponsorship to climb Everest and spent months making cold calls and trying to set up meetings. In the end, she got her sponsor and was successful on the mountain – it seemed like a fairy tale. 'You can do it,' she said, looking me in the eye. 'If I can do it, so can you.' It was just what I needed to hear. I went home, re-invigorated to keep trying.

As February 2010 approached, pure panic started to set in. I was frustrated with my injury and, after countless phone calls and emails to companies across the UK, I was no closer to finding a sponsor. I knew it had taken J. K. Rowling twelve rejections from publishers before *Harry Potter* had finally been picked up by Bloomsbury, but I had submitted hundreds of sponsorship requests and so far I had got nowhere. *Maybe this is impossible*, I started to think.

For nearly five months I had clung to the hope that, if I stuck to the formula – worked hard, didn't give up and kept putting my proposals out there – eventually I'd find a sponsor, but it hadn't worked. I was in exactly the same position as I had been when I had arrived home from Manaslu, except now I had a training injury and a huge phone bill to pay.

I thought about throwing in the towel almost every hour of the day. Each embarrassing cold call was another nail in the Everest coffin, every email proposal receiving no response a glaringly obvious message that, to everyone else, Everest wasn't interesting or important. I started to see that nobody else was ever going to be as excited about my future as I was. I needed to be the driving force, but somewhere along the way, my energy to keep going was dwindling. On training runs I'd started asking myself, *What's the point in training for a mountain I'm never going to climb?*

In my lowest moments, I would ask, *Why am I putting myself through this?* Thankfully, I could always answer that question. I learnt to spend time reminding myself of why I had started on this journey in the first place. I would lie in bed and visualise the climb ahead, toiling with the mountain and with my team, giving it everything I had; falling to my knees on the top of the world, looking up and seeing the curvature of the Earth. Each night, I'd fall asleep with these visions in my mind and say to myself, *I can't give up on this just because I don't want to make any more cold calls tomorrow.* Taking a moment to remind myself of the bigger picture gave me the perspective I needed when my nose was up against the grindstone, and even small things suddenly felt overwhelming. *I'm just going to try again tomorrow*, I'd say to myself as I drifted off. Ultimately, that was the only thought that mattered.

Fortunately, that 'tomorrow' finally came on 2 February 2010. The day before that though, on 1 February, Kenton had rung me to say that time was running out. 'I'm really sorry Bonita, but if you can't get the funds sorted by the end of the week, you can't come on the trip.'

I put the phone down in stunned silence. After all this work, all this promise and this huge dream that felt so alive, it had all come to nothing. It was over. I knew after all this time, I couldn't live in a dream world any more. Time had caught up with me; that's the thing about dreams, they don't factor in how fast time slips away.

I lay in bed that night, the stark silence hanging like truth in the air. It was written in the stars all along. I had indeed followed a fool's errand. *How had I not seen it? Did I really honestly think that little old me would be able to do this? Who did I think I was? The facts were plain to see, and everyone else around me could see them, why couldn't I? What was wrong with me?*

The world felt like a cold and cruel place. Reality, unlike my vivid daydreams, was grey and sober. My legs were aching from training that evening, my body exhausted from months of being pushed so hard. For the first time in nearly two years, I fell asleep dreaming not about lofty summits, but about the impending reality that the next few months were going to be nothing out of the ordinary. I went to sleep feeling like an utter failure.

The next morning, my alarm buzzed, signalling that it was time for a morning run. I looked at my phone and thought, *What's the point? What's the point in training for a mountain that I'm never going to climb? I haven't found the money in the last five months; I'm not going to find it in the next few weeks.* And with that, I rolled over and tried to go back to sleep.

Is this it then? The voice said in my head. *All this effort, and you can't be bothered to get out of bed? What happened to seizing the day? Everest climbers seize the day; they don't stay in bed. Maybe you are a failure, after all.*

'Right!' I said aloud. One more day. Tomorrow I give up. This is it. One last day and then I'm getting on with my life.

If I hadn't got out of bed that morning, I wouldn't be writing this now.

Like every morning on my drive to Swinley Forest, I would listen to Capital Radio in the car. This one particular morning, my mind desperately searching for an answer in the dying moments of my sponsorship search, a light bulb suddenly lit in my head.

Call the radio station!

I pulled into Swinley Forest car park and dialled the number that they read out on air for listeners' calls. Incredibly, I managed to persuade the producer to let me be interviewed live on air by the breakfast show presenters Lisa Snowdon and Johnny Vaughan. I can't remember a single thing we spoke about, and after thirty seconds they cut me off.

My phone was shaking in my hand from nerves, and I realised I'd probably just been broadcast to over a million people across the UK. *Maybe someone heard who might sponsor me*, I thought. After everything I'd been through, I knew not to get my hopes up. It was at least worth getting out of bed for. *A good start to the day.* With that, I chucked my phone in the glove box, and headed out on a frosty morning run with Belinda.

I told Belinda about the radio interview, but also that Kenton had given me a final deadline, and that it would be almost impossible for me to find the sponsorship in time. 'Well, Bonnie, what an amazing experience. Think of how far you've come – and there's always next year.' She was right, there was always next year, and she was right too about how far I'd come. Never in my life did I think I would be interviewed on Capital FM!

The forest was icy and majestic. As we ran through frosted ferns and glittering spider webs, I felt a kind of peace come over me. Whatever happened, I had so much to thank Everest for. Everest had given me a lease of life. It had energised me to get out of bed every day and work towards something that was meaningful to me. I had thrived on the challenge, and felt truly proud of myself for not giving up in so many moments when I thought I had nothing left to give.

Reflecting on the last five months was bittersweet. I hadn't realised how much courage I had until I started this journey, and while on the surface it had seemingly come to nothing, I felt as though I had come out of this experience better for it.

I thought that perhaps I had already lived some of the dream. I had got to live the dream of being an Everest aspirant, on the sponsorship circuit and training every day. I had climbed Mount Manaslu and met so many new friends and been to so many new places that I would otherwise never have seen. Everest, despite being thousands of miles away, had given me so much more than I could ever have expected. I was glad to have given in to its tremendous pull. Did I have any regrets? None at all.

Back at my car a few hours later, I grabbed my phone and saw that there were loads of missed calls and messages from friends who had heard me on the radio. As I scrolled through, my phone rang. I didn't recognise the number. 'Bonita it's Mark, Mark Chapman from VocaLink,' said the voice down the phone when I picked up.

I had been in talks with VocaLink about sponsoring me for a while, but so far they hadn't been able to come up with all the funds I needed. 'Oh hi Mark!' I said, trying not to sound so out of breath.

'Hiya. Yeah so, a lot of us heard you on the radio this morning. We were really impressed. I've spoken to my team and we've decided that we'd like to offer you all the money you need to go and climb your mountain, provided that the next time you get on national radio, you mention us … Is that OK? Bonita?'

I can't remember the rest of that conversation. But I do remember driving home with tears streaming down my face thinking, *Dreams really can come true, if you don't give up when you most want to.*

A few days later, VocaLink had transferred the sponsorship funds to my bank account, and I had walked up to HSBC in Wokingham to make the transfer to my team. When I saw my bank balance come up, it read £50,012. The £12 was obviously all I had in my account. That moment was probably one of the proudest moments of my life. To anyone else, it would have looked as if that money had been magicked out of nowhere. But it wasn't magic. It was hard work, and not giving up when I most wanted to. Finding that sponsorship had nothing to do with making me a better climber, but with any challenge in life, there are always going to be obstacles in the way. These obstacles can either become an excuse, a reason that you gave up, or they can become part of the challenge itself. Perhaps you might even write a book one day about how you didn't give up when you most wanted to.

People often say that I was lucky to get sponsored to climb Mount Everest. Those same people are often wearing shoes. They are clothed, and they have jobs and cars and houses, and they are telling me that I am lucky. If you have the ability to purchase this book and the time to read it, you too are probably one of the luckiest people to have ever been born in the history of humankind.

When people say that to me, I ask them, 'What are you doing with your luck?' The greatest luck of all is the lottery of birth. Of course I'm lucky. And I feel duty-bound to make the most of that luck.

But was it VocaLink that contacted me asking if they could offer sponsorship? No. Did Capital FM call me for that interview?

When I first started my journey towards Everest, I had never climbed a mountain and I didn't have two pennies to rub together. I hope my story goes to show that you can make your own luck in life. That it doesn't matter where you come from, with perseverance and a little self-belief, anything can happen. Often, just getting out there, into the world, is what's important. That's where opportunities arise and you learn who you want to be in life. But my dad and my family were so right all along – it's the people who don't give up who make it. Often, the difference between success and failure is simply the fact that one person gave up when the other didn't. I think back to that first phone call I made to the receptionist all those months previously. Most people would never have made that call. From that first call, to the one I made in desperation to Capital FM, most people wouldn't have picked up the phone. I learnt then that I always wanted to be the person who picked up the phone, who went above and beyond and who had the attitude, 'What's the worst that can happen?'

I read a quote once that always stayed with me: 'Do something right now that your future self will thank you for.' Writing this now as my 'future self', I can't believe what I actually put myself through at the time. I am so impressed by my twenty-one-year-old self. By her determination and resilience; by how she picked herself off the floor so many times and carried on. I did so many things based on nothing more than the *hope* that if I kept trying, eventually I would get somewhere. Hope was all I had. I am so thankful that my twenty-one-year-old self had enough courage to realise that hope alone was enough. And the foresight to realise that whatever reasons and excuses she could find for why Everest would never happen, she also knew that it was her and her alone who would have to deal with letting those excuses win. When it comes to our wildest dreams, there are no excuses. You either sacrifice living your life for your dreams, or you sacrifice your dreams to live your life. The choice is yours.

The money was gone from my account a few seconds later. I was back to having £12 to my name. I couldn't have cared less about my financial situation. A few days before

I had been running through Swinley Forest, grateful that Everest had led me to discover so much about the world, despite the fact that I would probably never see the mountain with my own eyes. Now, I was all set to be a real Everest mountaineer, and was off to face that mountain all the way to the highest point on planet Earth. To battle through minus 40°C temperatures, ice storms and knee-deep snow.

Was I lucky? I thought I was the luckiest girl in the world.

I stared around at the explosion of kit in my bedroom. Piles of thermal leggings and long-sleeved Icebreaker tops, goggles, spare goggles, a huge pile of medicines, a heap of brightly coloured down – a down suit, jacket, trousers, gilets – plus the hardwear: spiky crampons, ice axes, ice screws and karabiners … And then there were the home comforts I was going to take: the hot-water bottle and furry cover imitating my cat that my mum had given me, photos of my brothers and sisters, lots of bars of Green & Black's chocolate from my dad, and good-luck cards and notes from my aunties and cousins.

Turning back to my diary, I found it so hard to put into words my feelings of what was about to happen – yes, I was staring at the kit I would be using to survive on Everest right in front of me, but everything had happened so fast that it still seemed too surreal to be a dream come true.

I managed to write:

This week has been different to what I expected – people keep asking: are you excited, nervous?! The answer is, I am so beyond excitement and nerves – the build-up for this trip has been nearly eighteen months long – I simply feel like it is time to go and do what I set out to; no big fanfare of emotion – just simply the final step in this incredible journey. I think 'focused' is the answer.

Bizarrely, I felt a sense of shutting down emotionally. When I saw my mum's eyes glaze over with tears, or my dad gave me an extra-tight hug, I knew they were almost overwhelmed by their feelings. My coping mechanism, surrounded by so much emotion, was to shut down. All I could think about at that stage was the mountain; like a moth to a flame, I was drawn without fear. I felt ready to accept my fate.

On the last night before I was due to leave, my mum threw a farewell dinner for our family. As usual with my family, the night went on late and everybody got very drunk. I stood in the corner of the kitchen next to the radiator and wished that everyone would leave. I felt so uncomfortable with the attention, with everyone celebrating me, even when I had done absolutely nothing. But, it was important to my mum, and that was the main thing. Somebody asked me for the hundredth time how I was feeling and I found myself saying, 'I'm just desperate to get on that plane.' It was the truth. I wanted nothing more than the peace of the mountains, where I could breathe.

I walked into the living room and saw everyone dancing to Michael Jackson, glasses above their heads. I smiled at how mad my family are. How did I become such a black sheep?

Somewhere amongst the group was my mum, no glass in hand, her head down and tears in her eyes. My cousin had an arm around her. To this day I can't imagine the resilience she had to muster to hold her head up, make the best she could of the situation, and do the only thing she thought she could do to help: throw a party. I am so proud of my mum for her strength, for her acceptance of her worst nightmare coming true, for ploughing on with a huge smile and lots of energy, managing – most of the time – to mask the sick feeling in her stomach. When she woke up the next day, with a raging hangover, I was gone. I can't imagine the silence as she sat up in bed and thought that she might never see her daughter again.

The next day, my dad drove me to the airport with my brothers. I slipped a card into the seat pocket for him. It read, 'Dad, I love you so much. Thank you for all your support, love Bons'.

All too soon, we were at the gates, all hugging goodbye. I kept seeing the entrance to security and I was desperate to step over that threshold; not because I didn't want to say goodbye, but because I felt so drawn to my fate – as if my whole life had been leading up to this moment. I broke away from the last embrace, and as I stepped around the corner and everyone disappeared from view, the thought crossed my mind that I might never see them again. I stamped it out immediately. I couldn't entertain thoughts like that.

CHAPTER 9

I arrived in Kathmandu in the humid, sticky twilight hour on 3 April 2010. The sun coughed out its last rays, turning the thick city smog into a feeble pink and grey. Despite the blanket of darkness, the city didn't slow at all. Cars raced past cows standing in the middle of the road, and thousands of locals and tourists from all over the world mingled in rubble-strewn streets, draped with a thousand electrical cables overhead. I breathed in the foreign air – incense, sweat and heat. It felt good to be back. Already, home felt so far away. I had that familiar feeling again – I wondered whether I'd ever go home again, or if this would be the last world I'd ever know.

I met up with my team for the first time at the Summit Hotel. First, Lynette from Australia. She was on Manaslu at the same time as me, climbing mostly with Guy Willet, Kenton's guiding partner, whilst I climbed mostly with Henry's team. She didn't make it to the summit because of an illness, but that hadn't deterred her from taking on Everest only a few months later. Lynette was in her forties and a kind and sweet person, who cared deeply about the people she encountered.

Then, there was Rick and his wife, Alma: Rick is an all-American dad and doctor, in his late forties, with a bristling beard and moustache. He seems like an archetypal church-going family man and upstanding member of his community. I instantly liked him and Alma, and thought he would be someone I could trust on the hill.

Then there was Tom, a bush pilot, and one of the most fascinating people I'd ever met. He'd spent most of his life flying his plane around the world, writing a journal for *National Geographic*. He'd escaped cannibals in the Central African Republic, bribed his way out of prison in Zimbabwe, and crash-landed his plane in the jungles of the Congo. Everest, to him, was just another stop on the adventure he calls life, a chance to pit himself against nature and come away with another illustrious tale. He always carried a notebook and pencil, and every time we met a Nepalese person, he asked them to tell him Nepalese phrases, which he scribbled down. In no time at all, he was chatting to everyone from the Sherpas to the school kids in their mother tongue.

Finally, there was David, a fellow Brit and a lawyer. He was in his sixties and had drunk in life to the full. He was highly motivated, pragmatic, energetic; someone who got things done. He was almost hyperactive in his interest in every conversation, and in the world around him.

In addition, joining us for the trek to Everest Base Camp at 5,300 metres were Mick and Lewis, both from the UK; I wished they were coming all the way to the summit with us. They were great fun, remaining in good spirits even after both getting food poisoning that first night in Kathmandu.

From Kathmandu, we flew to Lukla. This was probably the most dangerous part of our trip: every year, on average, a plane crashes taking off or landing on the runway strip that drops straight off the side of the Khumbu Valley. Luckily our flight went without trouble and we landed on the runway, rocketing towards the mountain in front of us before suddenly swerving and coming to a halt.

Leaving the air-strip, we entered yet another world – this one composed of yak dung, cobbled stone paths and freshly painted new lodges. The tourism business was booming. Beyond the shadows of the buildings were snow-capped peaks that shined brilliant white in the glaring sun. I was instantly calmed by the relative peace of the Khumbu Valley in comparison to Kathmandu. No more traffic, no more street noise; now all we had to do was start walking.

Ahead of us was a ten-day trek through the Khumbu Valley up to Everest Base Camp, at 5,300 metres. These days were crucial for our acclimatisation. We had to make sure that we arrived in Base Camp fresh and feeling in the best shape possible. Get beaten down here, with sickness, bad blisters, even just dehydration, and you were committing yourself to a tough climb ahead. Turn up to Base Camp feeling strong, however, and you would be increasing your chances of getting to the summit greatly. Unfortunately, one of the team began to suffer from the effects of altitude almost as soon as we arrived. David, the British lawyer, despite having trained so hard, could not acclimatise. It doesn't matter how hard you've trained or how fit you are – if your body doesn't want to acclimatise, then there's pretty much nothing you can do. David struggled on, unable to sleep each night. It's a wonder he managed to make it to Base Camp: that represents serious mind over matter.

Two days into the trek, I wrote in my diary:

We are currently at an altitude of 3,460 m. Already seen a guy suffering from altitude sickness get taken to hospital on a donkey. I know if I ascend too fast here it could be a death sentence ...

Fortunately, I felt fine, acutely aware of what my body was going through, having pushed it all the way into the death zone on Mount Manaslu. The most important acclimatisation phase the human body goes through takes place at around 3,000 metres. Here, it is most vital to give your body time to adapt to the lack of oxygen in each breath, while it has the energy to recover and create more red blood cells. I knew that if I could acclimatise well here, below Base Camp, then I should have built a strong foundation of red blood cells that would continue to multiply as I headed closer to the summit.

A few days later, we found ourselves at the Tengboche Monastery, at nearly 4,000 metres. I took off my shoes and padded into one of the internal chambers, where wooden panels are gilded in golden and red paint. We sit on the floor with our backs against the wall. Incense hangs thick in the air, and light dapples through the small windows, catching the floating dust in its rays. Rows of monks sit on wooden benches, hunched over sacred texts in their deep-maroon robes. One keeps the beat of the ethereal chanting by hitting a gong that builds the rhythm into a climax. The chanting is hypnotic.

I lean back against the wooden wall, which is emblazoned with paintings of dragons and other mythical creatures, and my eyes close. I find myself sinking into a different state altogether. The chanting is building to a fever pitch. The smoky, warm monastery is replaced by a vivid daydream:

I'm walking to the summit of Everest. I can see prayer flags. The wind and snow blow across my face. I'm walking so slowly, but I'm going to make it – step by step. The prayer flags flutter in the wind. I'm alone on the summit. I feel a deep sense of peace come over me and one word comes to my mind: trust. Someone, somewhere, is telling me to keep my faith.

Days later, I was at Sonam's Lodge in Pangboche at 4,810 metres. It was 6.30 a.m. Even just standing still, I could feel my heart beating twice as fast as usual. We were, by scientific classification, at 'extreme' altitude, even though we were still hundreds of vertical metres lower than Everest Base Camp. The sheer magnitude of the expedition was becoming clearer every day.

The Khumbu Valley – and my teammates – were just starting to stir. There was a chill still weighing heavy in the air and I clasped a cup of milky tea in my gloved hands. I leant forwards on the brightly painted wooden balcony rails outside the lodge doors. I had a clear view of a black mountain miles away. The highest peak on Earth, Mount Everest.

The Great Sagarmatha, I thought, staring, unblinking, taking in every inch of the Mother Goddess of the Sky. I had seen this mountain in so many pictures, but now I felt as if I knew it intimately. It felt as though I'd been waiting my whole life to see it.

As I looked up to the distant summit I thought, *What on Earth will happen to us up there?*

I noticed the vapour of my breath: I was breathing deeply, my lungs unconsciously drawing in more oxygen, steadying a sudden release of adrenaline. My brow furrowed as I tried to read my future in the mountain. I imagined a group of humans battling their way to the top, so fragile in comparison to this mighty beast. I thought about how tiny my beating heart was, how thin the layer of skin was that protected my bones. I had never felt more humbled and more ill at ease in the face of nature, confronted by my own mortality.

I just could not imagine stringing the entire expedition together, surviving all the millions of deadly possibilities that it presented, the time away from home, missing family. My chest tightened. The voices in my head started up: *You'll never make it.*

I remember a strong sense of identifying the thoughts that would be my enemy, and those that would be my allies in the struggle ahead. I told myself to always remember that when I felt my chest tighten again, helpless in the face of this mighty monster (the monsters of my imagination, more than the monsters of the mountain), I would remind myself of this simple fact: you cannot control more than the next minute of your life.

I told myself: you aren't going to the summit today. You're not even going to the mountain. Today, all you have to do is make it to Dingboche village.

Any effort I make today might feel like a drop in the ocean, but I have to trust that it will all add up; that this day's trekking to Dingboche is as important as the last day towards the summit. *Just do everything you can now to look after yourself, so that when the summit comes, you're in the best shape possible.*

I gulped down more of the steaming, sickly-sweet milky

tea in my hands and tried to accept the hardships ahead. I looked at the impossibility of Everest, and through the dread settling over me, there was a tingling of excitement: *What if you do make it?*

I didn't dare to imagine being successful for more than a moment. I couldn't imagine ever being that lucky.

On one of the final days of trekking to Base Camp, I joined Mick and Lewis (who were only going as far as Base Camp), to climb up a small peak called Chukhung-Ri. As we collapsed in a heap of sweat at 5,440 metres, we could survey the whole Khumbu Valley around us. I looked out to peaks like Ama Dablam and Lhotse, and was so struck by their majesty. It wasn't the first time that I had felt like the luckiest person in the world, looking out at such a view, and the thought rose in my mind: *I wonder if I'll ever climb one of those peaks one day?*

As we sat there, our chests rising and falling, our bodies scrambling to adapt to the altitude, I felt strong. I knew that every time I pushed my body, it fought back. All my training was so far paying off. We sat on the summit of Chukhung-Ri until the mountain chill settled in our bones; then it was time to get up and run down the scree back to the lodge for dinner. Before we left, I scratched the names of my siblings into pieces of rock: *Ollie, Ben, Sean, Harry, Alfie and Emily*. I propped up each individual stone so that it too could survey the amphitheatre of mountains. For a moment, home felt close again.

A day later we found ourselves trekking through the Everest

memorial. Lines of stone memorials stood along a ridge like soldiers as we trekkers passed through their midst. Sleet and fog swept through, only allowing us the briefest glimpse of the words etched into each memorial. Reams of prayer flags blew silently. It is said that the prayers on the flags are swept up in the wind and sent to the gods. I thought I could hear their silent respects. As the mist swirled around me, I felt the dead tightening their grip, pulling me back. What right did I have to keep going? I moved quickly. I didn't stop. I feared that if I lingered too long, I would become one of them.

A grave reminder of the dangers of altitude struck en route to Lobuche.

We were having tea in our lodgings when a distressed British man came in; he was vomiting and looked on the verge of unconsciousness. Kenton ran out of the lodge with his sat phone to call a helicopter, while Dr Rick assessed the man and tried to find out what was wrong.

We assumed altitude sickness. His face was swollen; he was dizzy. He could have an advanced cerebral oedema, and in that case he could die at any moment. Kenton came back with a bottle of oxygen and then ran out again to speak on the sat phone. The bottle was left on the table with the regulator and mask, and everybody looked at it and then at each other – does anyone know how to set this up?

I grabbed the canister and twisted the regulator on to the opening; a sharp hissing noise exploded and I kept spinning the regulator until the hissing air was trapped. Then, I linked up the oxygen mask to the regulator and slid the mask over the man's deathly white face. We turned up the oxygen flow to over 4 litres per minute, and within a few breaths we could see that the man was starting to relax – even just the placebo effect of oxygen was miraculous. Moments later, he ripped off the mask and ran outside to projectile-vomit again. Thankfully, the helicopter soon arrived and he was whisked away to the metropolis of Kathmandu, his shocked team left wondering how on earth his health could have deteriorated so quickly. As I looked at his forlorn crew, I felt so thankful that my team were so competent and could take charge in the moments when it mattered most.

On 14 April, after ten days of trekking, we were on our final approach to Base Camp. Dusty paths gave way to glacial ice, while above us there loomed thousands of boulders, waiting for their moment to crash down through the lines of trekkers like skittles. We could see the debris across our paths. I didn't want to stop. I wanted the safety of camp, of my tent, and a nice cup of cold fruit tang. It had been a long and hot morning. I was so glad I wasn't covered in hair like the poor yaks that staggered past.

Hundreds of porters passed us, each carrying a 23-kilo load to Base Camp. I stood head and shoulders above all of them, and their ankles and arms were so delicate. I thought I was strong, but when I saw these people carrying what looked like over half their body weight for up to five hours a day, I realised that I was not strong at all. If these porters got the chance to climb Everest, I thought, they would leave all of us for dust.

Walking into Everest Base Camp was like walking into

a whole new world. There were around a thousand people, maybe three or four hundred climbers, plus their support crews. There were walkie-talkies going off, Sherpas hanging out, playing cards, water boys lugging water between the tents. It was a riot of colour: yellow, orange and blue tents, bright jackets, clashing trousers. Everyone was wearing sunglasses and had a little sunburn on their cheeks. It was lively, full of energy: there was so much uncertainty and yet so much promise. It was the beginning of the season; everyone was full of hope and excited to get stuck in.

Kenton led us to our Base Camp, and Kami, our Sirdar (guide), greeted us, alongside Bhim, who had been on Manaslu. It was so great to see him and his huge smile again. We collapsed into our mess tent. Home for the next six weeks. There was an odd silence in the team, but I imagine we were all thinking the same thing: *This is it. We're here.*

CHAPTER 10

Our camp was on the top of a ridge, looking down on a tent city that stretched for a kilometre into the shadows of Everest itself. Up here, we had our own private little village. We had a cook tent that was dark, smoky, built of stones, and then finished with a blue tarpaulin over the top. I would sometimes duck into the tent to say hello to Bhim and the cook boy, Hemanta, and get a cup of hot, sweet Sherpa tea.

The mess tent was a few paces away and somewhat brighter and airier – it had a big table running down the middle, and on the table there were pots and jars of everything from peanut butter to Branston pickle. Kenton had bought a huge wheel of cheese, and at 4 p.m. the team would get the cheese out and sit playing Monopoly and chatting for hours, listening mostly to Tom's sometimes unbelievable stories about his travels through Africa as a bush pilot.

Our individual Ozark tents surrounded the mess tent, and every night we would head off with our head torches, looking for our own tents, and on more than one occasion stumbling into the wrong one, only to wake up a disgruntled teammate. After dinner, we would brush our teeth outside in the bitter cold. Not speaking, we would look down at our kingdom. Base Camp was speckled with orange tents lit up by their inhabitants' head torches, and above that we could see the jagged spires of the mountains, and beyond those the deep-blue sky and a billion stars.

In my tent, I had a blow-up Therm-a-Rest on a thick woven rug, and a minus 20°C sleeping bag. I'd sleep with the hot-water bottle that my mum had given me, and I had my university hoodie with 'RHUL' emblazoned across it, which I stuffed into a ball and used as a pillow. It was blissfully cosy. Sometimes, before going to sleep, I would allow myself to think of home, but only for a few seconds before shutting those kinds of thoughts out again.

A few days after arriving at Base Camp, we had our Puja ceremony. A Puja is a Buddhist ceremony to bless each climber and ask the gods for safe passage on the mountain. The ceremony itself went on for over two hours. A local monk chanted endless prayers from ancient scriptures; another beside him bashed a drum and chanted along too. We drank Chang, a home-brewed spirit, and lots of beer. I placed my climbing boots and ice axe at the Puja to be blessed, hoping that the pieces of equipment wouldn't fail me on the mountain when I needed them most. The ceremony finished with everyone throwing rice in the air as a final thanks to the mountain for bringing us together.

Finally, I got to catch up with Rob Casserley. He had just come off his Atlantic row. His hair was almost shoulder-length, his face red and weathered by months of surviving completely self-sufficiently on the ocean. Again, Rob's resilience never ceased to amaze me. I couldn't believe that he still had the scars on his legs from the sores caused by rowing, day in day out, in the salty air, and yet he was here on Everest, on a trip for which the rest of us had carefully prepared for months. It was a true testament to Rob's character and incredible strength that he could go from one hideous challenge to another.

The Sherpa team teased Rob for his long, matted hair. It was great to hang out with them again and listen to the endless banter. Our team comprised Dorjee, Lhakpa Wongchu, 'Young' Lhakpa, Jabu, Namgel and Thundu. Kami, our Sirdar, was in charge, and there to ensure their safety on the mountain. It goes without saying that without these men, none of us would have a hope of getting to the summit. They and the other Sherpa teams were the backbone of Everest. They brought the mountain to life. For the most part, we would not climb with them, but just pass them on the hill as they fixed ropes higher up and carried loads of oxygen, gas and other equipment. It was only when summit day came that we would each be paired together, like scuba-diving buddies, as we climbed through the death zone, breathing artificial oxygen on a 15-hour round trip from Camp Four.

I felt so inadequate compared to these mountain men. They were so fast, so strong and so fearless. But they were – of course – still human, and they got exhausted, cold and scared like the rest of us. It was just that they rarely showed it. Their stoicism was probably their defining characteristic. I hated seeing them get treated badly by the odd egotistical climber, and nothing made my stomach churn more than seeing Sherpas serving tea in bed to other teams. To me, that morning ritual was totally unnecessary, and set a tone of inequality that I believe in its small way eventually led to the Sherpa unrest a few years after my ascent.

I also feel awkward writing this and referring to them as Sherpas, as a considerable number of these high-altitude climbers are not even from the Sherpa region of Nepal or Tibet. However, in the nearly 100 years since Everest first began to be explored and climbed, the foreigners and locals have not been able to find a better way to distinguish themselves. So, for lack of a better word, I will refer to the indigenous climbers as Sherpas. Perhaps in time the Everest community will come up with something better. Nothing else seems to encapsulate what a Sherpa does: they are not just porters, or guides, rope-fixers or rescuers; they are all of those things and so much more. I think that's why the name Sherpa has stuck, because nothing else comes close to describing the relentless work that the indigenous workers do, their incredible skills and the risks that they take.

In amongst the Sherpas, I noticed David. He was still struggling with the effects of altitude. 'I just can't sleep,' he said when I asked how he felt. 'As soon as I doze off, I wake up a minute later gasping for air. It goes on all night.' David's eyes were heavy and his demeanour had changed. He looked nothing like the strong guy who had turned up in Kathmandu only two weeks beforehand.

Looking into David's bloodshot eyes, I couldn't see how he would make it to the summit. If your body wasn't adapting down here, then up in the death zone it would be near impossible. I felt for him. Yes, perhaps he had been foolish coming straight to Everest with no prior experience on an 8,000-metre peak, but still – he had the same dream that I did. How would I have felt if the same cruel twist of fate had come my way?

Still, it was early in the expedition, and David wasn't going to give up that easily. We were planning on heading up the mountain the next morning, and as sure as hell, if David could keep taking those steps, he would.

That night, tucked into my sleeping bag in my tent, I listened to the distant chorus of avalanches and the cracking of the glacier beneath me. I couldn't sleep. Just beyond the tent wall was the Khumbu Icefall and, in a few hours' time, we were planning to head into it.

The Khumbu Icefall was our gateway to Everest. It was a glacier that cascaded down from one valley into another below, like a river becoming a waterfall as it hits steeper ground. It lay like a slackened mouth, thousands of tonnes of ice churning down the mountain, waiting for us humans to climb on to its tongue and march into the belly of the beast.

I gripped my hot-water bottle tightly and prayed to the universe: *Please don't let me die tomorrow.*

When I awoke the next morning at 4 a.m., I told myself to think about nothing more than putting my boots on and taking that first step out of the tent. I knew that if I could just get moving, the anxieties of the night before would start to fall away.

Base Camp was a frozen wonderland in the clutches of a deep sleep. Our Sherpa team had lit juniper branches and placed them by the Puja, to wish us safe passage on the mountain. The eerie golden flames and smoke drifted across Base Camp as we slowly trudged to crampon point. The fragrant smoke filled my lungs. Suddenly, all my dreams were to become reality – I was about to step on to Mount Everest for the first time.

I followed Kenton's footsteps closely. After 1 hour and 15 minutes we reached our first resting point. As we gulped down water, Kenton explained that we could mark the time we had before the sun hit us by keeping an eye on Mount Pumori, a peak on the opposite side of Base Camp. We could see that the very tip of Pumori had turned a blazing orange. As the sun rose, the light would move down Mount Pumori, across Base Camp and then up the icefall. We had about four hours until blazing-hot temperatures hit us. We needed to get out of the icefall before then, or risk snow blindness and, of course, the weakening of the already precarious ice from the intense heat.

For many hours we seemed to be the only team in the icefall. Head torches were put away as the sky turned pink. Pumori was becoming ever more orange as the sun rose threateningly. I was almost praying for its rays to hit us – I was so cold. My hands and nose were frozen.

My lungs heaved as I stomped up ice tracks and pulled myself over huge seracs. I almost wanted to pull back from the exertion, give myself a moment to catch my breath and stop the pain building but, at the same time, something told me I could keep going. I relished the rhythm and holding my body at that threshold. It was the same feeling that I got running as a girl: knowing that I could 'lean in' to the pain.

As I climbed up vertical walls of ice, jumped across crevasses, teetered around icicles, walked along ridges with huge drops either side, I felt incredibly grateful for what Rob and Henry had taught me on Mount Manaslu. The icefall felt less of a daunting place because of their mentorship.

Still, I felt an intense respect for the power of the ice. It could take my life away in an instant. A serac the size of a house could collapse, or a weak snow bridge could give way beneath my feet.

I caught up with Kenton and Rick taking a rest. I opened my mouth to say hello, but the cold had numbed my face so much that all that came out was a slur. We couldn't help but laugh at how frozen we all looked.

As we climbed higher, the terrain became more precarious and dangerous. Prayer flags marked the most deadly sections. I almost wished the flags weren't there; my ignorance would have kept me much calmer. Then I went around a corner and came face to face with my first ladder crossing. My first leap of faith.

The crevasse was over 4 metres wide. Its jaws were a brilliant blue, with millions of sparkling crystals imprisoned in the ice. Then the blue turned to black. There was no way of knowing how deep the crevasse was. It looked as though it wanted to swallow me whole.

Our only passage over it was a metal ladder laid across from one side to the other, attached by ropes fixed into the ice with metal stakes. The icefall doctors, as they are known, a team of Sherpas who had gone ahead of the rest of the teams at Base Camp and fixed a route through the icefall, would have put this ladder in place. The ladder was chipped and scarred from all the years of heavy-booted mountaineers trampling across it. It was no more than two footprints wide. Now I had to trust it with my life.

I grasped the ropes on either side of the ladder and leant forward as far as I dared, as if in a kind of ski-jump formation, with my arms behind me, holding on to the ropes. My face loomed over the ladder and the dark crevasse gaped open. *Lean in*, I told myself. I knew that the more I leant forward, the more secure I'd become. I felt utterly exposed standing there, in flux, ready to go and yet totally unable to move. I looked over the edge again and thought, *I can't do this.*

The ladder crossing was not a physical challenge. There were far more technically and physically demanding challenges ahead. This was a mental battle. I tried to stay composed, and to reason with the fatalistic voices in my head, but they were screaming at me: *You are definitely going to trip up and die here!*

I leant back, and the ropes I was holding slackened. Now, my heart was really pounding. *Everest was never going to be easy*, I told myself. *You can do this; you've done harder things on Manaslu. Just trust yourself and take a leap of faith!*

I decided that my only option was to try and block everything out, and focus all of my energy on to nothing more than lifting my foot off the ground. My attention was so focused on the detail of my boot, I wouldn't allow my line of sight to stray from the colour of my shoelace. If I could focus wholly on nothing more than the simple process of lifting up my foot, then I wouldn't be so scared.

I needed to stop thinking, and just do. *Focus on the detail. Focus on the process.*

Somehow, I managed to mechanically lift my foot and place it on to the ladder. With that, my other foot followed. I tried to ignore the squeals of the ladder as it groaned under my weight, and the teeth of my crampons screeching as they awkwardly locked into the metal rungs. *Lean in.* I took another step, and another. *Focus on the process.*

I couldn't see anything in my peripheral vision but blackness. My chest tightened again. I was totally suspended. As I lifted my leg, I realised how violently it was shaking. *Focus*, I told myself. It took all my concentration to move carefully. Every movement was a chance to lose balance and fall. *Focus on the detail.*

I took a final step off that ladder, and back on to solid ice. I was so relieved it was over, and yet immediately I thought to myself, *What on earth were you making such a fuss about?*

That's the thing about leaps of faith. Before we take them, we believe we are facing the most terrifying situation in the world. When we look back once they are over, we often realise that we were more than capable all along. If climbing has taught me one thing, it's that I won't ever overcome fear; fear will always be with me. But what I can do is block fear out, by focusing on something that doesn't scare me, by focusing on the process and the details of the next small step. Climbing has taught me that when I'm most scared, I should stop thinking and just *do*.

Eleanor Roosevelt said, 'Do one thing every day that

scares you.' The things I am most proud of in my life today are the things that have come from me pushing myself to do stuff that scared me. Doing things that scare me makes me realise what I am truly capable of, and that is often far more than what the voices in my head would let me think.

So I brushed myself down, and carried on up the icefall – there were twenty more ladders to cross before I would make it to the top. I tried not to think too much about the mammoth task ahead. *One step at a time*, I reminded myself.

The top of the icefall was marked by three vertical ladders tied together by rope and hung over an ice cliff. The moment I came over the final lip of the icefall, the sun burst into view and its warmth flooded through me as I took my first look at the Western Cwm. I felt so lucky to witness such a sight.

A glacier half a kilometre wide swept down from Everest, Lhotse and Nuptse, a red carpet of ice leading us directly to the highest point on Earth. Its surface rippled like a tongue, cracked and gaping in some places from crevasses that no ladder could stretch across. These crevasses were so big that we would have to climb down into them, find snow bridges within their depths, and then climb up the walls on the other side.

Either side of the glacier were majestic walls of rock, rocketing almost vertically into the sky. I was walking in the footsteps of Tenzing Norgay and Edmund Hillary. *In the footsteps of giants*, I thought. The Western Cwm is completely cut off from the rest of planet Earth. It is only accessible to humans via the treacherous Khumbu Icefall, or, in modern times, specially adapted helicopters. To just stand there and witness the scale and benign power of these mountains was the most humbling moment of my life. Knowing that I was one of the few people in the history of humankind to be in the presence of such beauty, and knowing the risks I'd taken to get there, made it that much more special.

The gentle walk to Camp One was glorious in comparison to the stress of the icefall. My team stopped many times just to take the scenery in. The first tents came into view soon after, which in our minds represented hot tea and warm sleeping bags. We arrived in good time at around 10 a.m. All in all, a five-hour ascent from crampon point was a great time for Rick, Tom and me. David and Lynette were still climbing below us. Kenton was happy; we were happy – we were at Camp One on Everest. I had to pinch myself again.

I was by default given the job of setting up Lynette's and my tent as I had arrived before her. The top priority was to collect a bagful of snow and melt it into drinking water.

Lynette arrived an hour later. I helped her take her boots off, arranged her sleeping mat and got her a hot drink. As we boiled water and sorted out our food for the night, the sunny weather outside disintegrated. A grey cloud settled itself over Camp One, snow began to fall and the wind began to howl.

The storm lasted all night. Wind pummelled the tent, and at one point I thought we would be blown away with the force. It was as if fifty men were punching and shoving the tent from every direction. I had also insisted on leaving the tent doors slightly open (for more oxygen circulation), meaning that we both woke up to spindrift – powdery snow – rushing into our warm chamber, covering our sleeping bags with a soggy layer.

As the sun rose, the winds did not abate. Lynette began boiling water at 5.30 a.m., and more than once a freak gust knocked over the stove, spilling the precious liquid everywhere. We could just about hear each other over the roar. Getting ready and packed to head back down to Base Camp took nearly two hours. Just stuffing my sleeping bag into its stuff sack at 6,000 metres took me about 15 minutes, as I needed so many breaks to catch my breath.

I told myself that for breakfast I would have a cup of tea and four custard cream biscuits. I managed three; my appetite had disappeared completely. Extra blood was being diverted to my brain, a survival mechanism that kicks in at altitude. Our brains need a constant large supply of oxygen, whereas other organs, our stomachs in particular, do not. Thus, our bodies cleverly divert blood supply from less vital areas to the brain, to keep feeding it the large amount of oxygen it needs. With not enough blood oxygenating my stomach, I couldn't digest food. This adaptation had left me feeling sick at the sight of food and not able to feel the hunger I should have felt after a five-hour climb the day before and only a few mouthfuls of soup for dinner. Climbers lose on average 10 per cent of their body weight during an Everest expedition. I lost that much in the first two weeks.

After my failed attempt at breakfast, the descent back

to Base Camp was soon under way. As I descended the ladders into the top section of the icefall, Tom caught up with me and we climbed down into the jumbled mess together. We edged around a serac, and beyond it we were met with an explosion of blue ice blocks covering our intended route. A dangerous-looking pinnacle of ice we had noticed the day before had evidently collapsed. Whilst I had marvelled at it from afar, Tom the bush pilot had sat underneath the pinnacle and said in his American drawl, 'I wonder how safe this is?'

Now, it was a car-crash of ice blocks, which had completely buried the fixed line under its shattered remnants. Kenton caught us up and shook his head at Tom. 'You are one lucky bugger!'

We made it back to Base Camp a few hours later. I took off my rucksack and let it fall with a thump to the ground. I then collapsed into a plastic chair and let out a huge sigh as the sun warmed my cheeks, my aching muscles finally able to relax. I realised that the altitude at Camp One hadn't affected me much – apart from the loss of appetite. We had made it safely up and down the mountain on our first foray. Everything was going to plan, I felt strong and the weather couldn't be better. I couldn't help but smile. Life was perfect.

Over the next three weeks, we planned to climb up and down the mountain, getting progressively higher with each climb. Now that we had reached Camp One, on our next journey we would go to Camp Two, then come back down again before heading up to Camp Three. We called these climbs 'rotations'. The reason for climbing and then retreating down again was so that we could continue to acclimatise.

Our bodies need time to adapt to stressful experiences. Take marathon training, for instance. If you've never run a step before, you don't turn up on race day ready to do 26 miles in one push – your body would probably give up less than halfway around the course, and you would be likely to get an injury. But running that same 26 miles can feel relatively comfortable if you've trained your body progressively over time from running that first step, then a mile, and eventually 20 miles.

Acclimatisation was essentially the same thing. Every time we climbed to a new height, our bodies were being exposed to less and less oxygen. The shock of this firstly triggered new red blood cells to be produced, and secondly left our bodies exhausted, meaning we would need to go down to more oxygenated air to recover. But when we came back to that height, it was not the same shock – our bodies had now created the red blood cells necessary to survive there, meaning we could push on a little higher until we were shocked again. If we repeated this process enough times, eventually we would be acclimatised enough to attempt the summit at 8,848 metres.

The most a human being can ascend in 24 hours when not acclimatised is around 1,000 metres. Any more, and we were extremely likely to contract a life-threatening cerebral or pulmonary oedema. If you don't train for a marathon, you can pull out halfway through; if you don't acclimatise properly on Everest, then you will most likely pay for that mistake with your life.

* * *

A few days later, on our way down from a rotation climb to Camp Two, I caught up with a group of climbers in the icefall. It was 10 o'clock in the morning, and the sun was baking down on the back of my neck. We were queuing to cross a ladder. As I awaited my turn, I heard a whimpering below me and a voice saying, 'Help me!' I looked down to see a woman on a ledge over a huge drop into a crevasse. She was trapped in a spider's web of ropes, asking everyone who passed her to help untangle her. Nobody stopped. I could see that she was starting to panic.

I knew what it was like to be that scared. I had been that woman on Manaslu: a nervous wreck; a total nightmare to deal with – not having enough mental resilience to pull myself together. I climbed down and tried to help.

As I helped her, we heard a huge *boom*, followed by a deafening crash. Out of the corner of my eye, I saw a massive block of ice collapse and fall into the depths of the crevasse I had been waiting to cross. Everybody ran in all directions, like ants escaping a stick prodded into their nest. I stood frozen, the woman crying next me. *Is the whole lot going to go? Is the ice underneath us going to collapse next?*

Adrenaline surged through my veins and sharpened my vision. I turned to her and grabbed her by the shoulders 'We have to get out of here, as fast as possible.' I could see that our best hope was to jump to another ledge, on the other side of the crevasse.

A climber barged past us to do the same. I saw the desperation in his eyes. Sherpas followed with the same expression on their faces, praying aloud as they rushed past us. I had never seen human beings so terrified. I watched with an odd detachment. I wasn't scared. I had a job to do.

'OK, we have to be quick, this is really dangerous! Jump and don't stop, carry on moving, OK?' I shouted.

The woman sobbed and shook her head, 'I can't.'

'Go!' I shouted. *Come on,* I thought, *you've got to help yourself.* I didn't want to die standing next to her, all because she couldn't find the will to move. I jumped across the crevasse to the ledge I hoped meant safety. 'Like this!' I shouted back to her. Now on her own, she finally managed to jump across, wanting to stay as close to me as possible. We held on to each other as we ran beneath more looming seracs, our feet padding on snow and ice, with crevasses dropping into darkness inches from our path. Finally, we reached a fixed line and I clipped us both to it. We collapsed into an exhausted heap. I could feel the adrenaline coursing through my body. My heart was racing so fast I felt it would burst from my chest.

Later, as I carried on climbing down, the woman just behind me, I ran through what had happened over and over in my mind. I had felt no fear at all. I had been paralysed by fear in so many situations and yet none of them had been as serious as that. It made me realise that sometimes the thing that allowed us to be most scared was the *time* we had to think. I didn't have time to be scared then. It made me think that if I have the time to feel scared about something, then it probably isn't as dangerous as I'm making it out to be. It made me think that perhaps we have to force ourselves to do things before we get too scared. That was the first time I'd had to make quick decisions in order to survive. My instincts had kicked in, as had my experience in the mountains. I knew that I was no longer the girl who had cried every day on Manaslu.

The next day we trekked two hours down to the nearest village, Gorak Shep, with David, who had realised he had no choice but to leave the expedition. He had not made it to Camp One on our first rotation, and his sleep apnoea hadn't improved. He had lost a lot of weight. Altitude had not been kind to his body. I was sad to see David go, though. He was always able to drum up everyone's spirits, despite how broken his were. He would look me in the eye and quite logically convince me that I was 100 per cent certain to reach the summit of Everest. Now he was gone, that positivity was definitely missing from our team.

After saying goodbye, I made the trek back to Base Camp alone. It felt good to go at my own pace. I went as fast as possible, feeling my lungs luxuriate in the 'thick' air down at 5,000 metres.

Within an hour I was back at the trekkers' shrine to Everest Base Camp, a plateau amongst the scree that looks down on Base Camp. It marked the entrance to camp for climbers, and gave the best views of our tent city for trekkers. There was an unwritten rule that trekkers were not supposed to pass this point, due to spreading coughs and colds that, if caught, could potentially ruin a climber's summit bid.

As I walked straight past the shrine and headed down the track towards camp, I was stopped by a trekking guide. 'Where are you going?'

'Base Camp.'

'Base Camp is for climbers only.'

'Yeah, I know.'

'Trekkers aren't allowed in.'

'Yes, I know.'

I carried on walking, and he shouted over, 'So what are you doing?'

I shouted back, 'Going home!' before turning and sliding out of sight down the scree towards Base Camp.

A few days later, I was toiling up the Lhotse face, headed towards Camp Three at 7,100 metres and not feeling at home by any stretch of the imagination. With every step, my body felt as though it was being split in half. The pain as I stabbed my boot into the ice exploded up my bruised and blistered toes, through my aching knees, and ripped up through my body, shuddering on my hip bones as the waist strap from my heavy pack rubbed my skin raw, and then a searing pain flooded into my upper back and my shoulders collapsed forwards, shutting my lungs off from being able to breathe properly. I knew this, but I just couldn't find the strength to stand up straight. Instead, I was bent double, gasping and dribbling into my hands as I grasped the fixed line and held on for dear life. A throbbing headache behind my brow, and salty sweat running into my stinging eyes topped everything off.

As I nearly collapsed forwards into the face again, I cursed myself for ever thinking that climbing the world's highest peaks was a good idea. *This is pointless.* One step felt so small and insignificant, yet so monumentally painful, that the thought of having to do thousands more felt insurmountable. I had hours more to go before reaching Camp Three. Overwhelmed and too exhausted to control my emotions, I started to feel hot tears well behind my eyes. *People like you don't climb mountains like Everest.*

As soon as the thought came into my head, I knew I had to prove it wrong. I reflected on the times on Manaslu when I'd floundered in the snow, begging for 'it' to be over. I wasn't quite sure what 'it' was, but I'm pretty sure I meant everything – the mountain, the pain, the feeling of being so overwhelmed, the dehydration, the homesickness. Everything. But still, I had found a way to keep going.

I looked down the Lhotse face and could see my little footprints, which had zigzagged upwards for nearly 400 metres. *They do add up*, I told myself. *They're not pointless.* I just had to trust the small steps. I had to stop focusing on how much I had left to do, and put all my faith into the next moment. *Everything else will sort itself out.*

I pushed on, telling myself over and over, *What doesn't kill you makes you stronger,* though I wasn't quite sure in that moment whether I believed myself or not, or whether I cared about getting stronger. All I cared about was that soon I would be at Camp Three and this would be a memory and I'd have a tomato Cup-a-Soup and then a hot chocolate.

When I did finally stagger into Camp Three a few hours later, I felt relief like I hadn't even felt after summit day on Manaslu. I had trusted the system, and it had worked. The small steps *did* add up to big things, and even when I felt as if I couldn't take another, I always managed to draw the strength from somewhere. If I could just keep taking those small steps, no matter how difficult each one was, then I was pretty sure I could make it to the summit of Mount Everest, if the great mountain herself permitted. I just had to focus everything I had on the next step.

The ledge where our tent was perched at 7,100 metres was less than 2,000 vertical metres from the summit of Everest. From our vantage point halfway up the expansive Lhotse face, we could see all the way down the Khumbu Valley towards Camps Two and One in the Western Cwm, then across Base Camp, up to Pumori, and then beyond Pumori the entire Himalayan range – mountains like Cho Oyu, the world's sixth-highest peak – sat assuredly on the horizon. I couldn't believe how high we were. Nor, looking back down to Base Camp, could I believe how far we'd come.

At that height on the mountain, our acclimatisation rotations would go no further. We would use bottled oxygen from that point onwards, due to the fact that the human body can barely acclimatise above 7,000 metres, as its ability to produce more red blood cells is almost at its limit.

We planned to spend the night there and then descend back to Base Camp to allow our bodies to recover. Once we were fit again and the weather was ready for us, we planned to try for the summit. It sounded easy, but so many things could go wrong in that time. Those next ten days or so would be the most crucial of my life.

I didn't want to leave my perch, sitting outside my tent on a tiny ledge, my feet swinging in thin air, the Lhotse face dropping beneath me. This glorious place, where the Himalayas laid themselves out before me. I could see for miles, I breathed the air, I smelt the air. Seven thousand metres is a special kind of place. I wondered whether I would ever stand at this spot again. *Would it all mean nothing if I didn't make it back here?* All the sweat and pain and exhaustion to climb to this point, only to leave, when the summit was seemingly so close.

Lynette had called it quits on that climb to Camp Three at 6,900 metres. She had fallen ill and had also been battling an ankle sprain that she had picked up when training in Australia. She packed her bags once we got back to Base Camp and flew back to Adelaide shortly after. Unfortunately, I was not surprised to see Lynette go, I felt she couldn't find a way to put in that last 10 per cent.

Lynette had done so much to get to her high point on Everest, just above Camp Two at 6,400 metres, but when push came to shove, when she was in pain, when she was hurting, when she was tired, she didn't seem to have the ability to push on through. Lynette had done everything, but she couldn't find a way to do the bit that mattered. A lot of people, me included, go so far out of our comfort zones, but as soon as we reach that real cliff edge, of unknown depths of despair and abject terror awaiting us, we pull back.

Most people never go the last 10 per cent. It's pretty easy to get to 90 per cent. Everyone can get to the point where they feel like they can't physically go on, but that's precisely the point when you have the choice to give up or keep going. If you want to achieve your wildest dreams, you have to keep on pushing; you have to find a way to take *one more step* – in spite of there apparently being every reason not to. There was no difference between Lynette and many of the other sick or injured climbers on Everest that year, except the choice they made when they reached

90 per cent. Some chose to keep pushing, others chose to give up. When it comes to achieving something that's difficult, the last 10 per cent is what counts the most. That magical last 10 per cent.

Still, Lynette waved us goodbye from Base Camp having had an experience that she would never forget, and that was worth a hell of a lot. Who cared if she didn't make it to the summit? She was a kind person with her heart in the right place, which was a lot more than could be said for some of the egos that had reached the top. And she would be back to try again, I was sure of it.

Our team had now dwindled to Tom, Rick the American doctor, and me, along with Kenton and the Sherpas. David and Lynette were homeward bound. I felt a pang of jealousy. Before I could think of home, I had the world's highest mountain to climb.

On 5 May 2010 I wrote in my diary:

> A very nerve-racking time at BC. Every time a weather report comes in we sit with bated breath to hear whether the summit of Everest continues to be battered by the jet-stream winds, or if the monsoon has pushed the winds north enough for us to sneak to the top – currently, we are still waiting.

I went to sleep that very night and woke at four in the morning to find my tent roof inches from my nose – it was weighed down with 4 inches of snow, and I could still hear the storm outside.

The inhabitants of Base Camp unzipped their tents on 6 May to a winter wonderland like no other. In the shadow of Mount Everest, there we stood, puffy-eyed in the snow, wearing our crocs and sandals and wondering where on earth the bloody lot had come from. It was deadly quiet.

After breakfast people milled around – and what do you instinctively do when surrounded by fresh, fluffy snow? Well, I started throwing it, and a huge snowball fight ensued.

The fight was ferocious and lasted well over an hour. Base Camp was perfect for such a fight – huge boulders to hide behind and more ammunition than we could ever need. There were ambushes and targeted assaults ... usually on me by six or more Sherpas.

Rob, who was good at everything, could throw a snowball for miles and was our team's main asset. I was more of a liability. But the true hero was Sundip, our team's water porter. His job was to collect water from a glacial pool and bring it back to Base Camp. He made this trip twenty times a day. But his true talent was in snowball fighting – his aim was spectacular and we all suffered from it.

Suddenly, after pelting us for an age, Sundip put his hands up and announced, 'Okay. I tired now,' and, just like that, the fight was over. We were all exhausted. Doing anything at 5,300 metres was tiring.

As we all collapsed in the mess tent, talk turned to the weather up high – we knew there and then that we wouldn't be going anywhere for a while.

Rob, Fi and James announced that they were heading down to Pangboche to stay at Sonam's Lodge with Sherpa friends that they knew well. Their reasoning was that the lower altitude would build their strength for the summit push.

I didn't think much more of their 'mini-break', as my team had said they would be staying put at Base Camp. I spent the day lying in my tent, reading *The Girl with the Dragon Tattoo*, when someone shouted, 'Oi, Norris!' It was Rob coming to say goodbye. I poked my head out of my tent, blinking into the searing-white snow, hair a mass of 'rats' tails', as my mum called them, to listen to Rob spin a story of comfy lodges with blankets and fires and lemon tea and fresh chicken. Plus, he told me I would build my strength back up at lower altitudes, as the oxygen-rich air would allow our bodies to recover from the exhaustion and few minor injuries and illnesses we'd all picked up. I was sold. I packed my bags there and then.

We set off: a bed, a shower and, most importantly, thick air awaited us.

We made it down to Pheriche in only a few hours. Every step was filling our lungs with more and more oxygen. I was loving it – my legs were moving! After days spent plonked in a chair or trapped in my sleeping bag, they were now dodging rocks and yak poo, striding up hills and jogging back down the other side. With the increased oxygen in the air I felt like a super-charged human. I couldn't seem to tire or get out of breath.

We made it to Sonam's Lodge in Pangboche after dark, and were greeted like old friends by Nima Lamu and Germin Sherpa. Settling down into the corner, we were warmed by the wood-burner, covered in blankets and fed *dal bhat*. I fell into a deep sleep that night, blissfully happy again.

I wrote in my diary, a few days into our stay at Sonam's:

Fi and I have done nothing but rest, read and eat. Fi's bronchitis has gone, and I am aiming to put on a pound a day as everyone keeps saying how much weight I've lost. We are basically preparing and fuelling our bodies for the summit push – six of the hardest days of our lives, plus a 17-hour marathon on summit day, the longest of my life.

We leave tomorrow (9 May) for the 15-mile walk back to Base Camp, which on the walk in took three days, but now we are acclimatised and fit, we will do in a one-day push.

People are talking about getting the summit 'over and done with'. I keep quiet. I am loving every minute of this expedition. What will be will be. I don't want to wish it away.

The next evening, having trekked 15 miles in one day back to Base Camp, I finally crawled into my tent, my legs aching and my body crying out for rest. Back at 5,300 metres' altitude, everything felt harder again. I felt strong and energised after my few days down in Pangboche, and my body was still acclimatised to nearly 7,000 metres, after we'd slept at Camp Three on our last rotation on the mountain. My team were asleep. We would be leaving at 4.30 a.m. to head into the icefall, not to return to Base Camp until after the attempt on the summit.

As I tucked myself into my sleeping bag, I heard a voice outside my tent. 'Didi, I have something for you.' It was Bhim. He had been waiting for me to arrive and had made me some *momos* for dinner. 'Thank you!' I said as he passed a plate of the hot dumplings into my tent. 'For energy,' he nodded. 'Need energy for summit.'

I shoved those dumplings into my mouth as though my life depended on it. With every mouthful I thought I would be sick. *This is it,* I told myself. *The small steps make the big difference.*

CHAPTER 11

'The sun watches what I do, but the moon knows all my secrets.'

J. M. Wonderland

In those first few steps away from camp, every exhausted cell in my body was begging me to get back in the tent, to sleep and recover. To not head into the darkness on the biggest marathon of my life. All the aches and pains that had subsided while I was sitting down had now begun screaming for my attention. I had never felt so weak. I was hyper-aware of the oxygen bottle digging into the back of my neck, every blistered patch of flesh being rubbed red raw again, my pounding heart and gasping lungs playing catch-up to the searing oxygen deficit that was building in my thighs. My pack swayed with the weight of its own gravity, rocking on my hip bones and trying to pull me from side to side. I gasped for air, drawing oxygen through the valves in my mask and into my lungs. The mask sucked on to my face. It felt as if it was trying to suffocate me. *I can't do this. I CAN'T DO THIS.* I wanted to rip off my goggles and mask and mittens and scream for help. I was trapped behind a barrier of clothing and kit that was pretending to protect me when all it was doing was weighing me down, killing me from inside. Every part of me was being stabbed and poked; every part of me was falling apart.

Through the nagging pain and my racing breath, I continued to walk in total silence. I kept lifting my legs; the lightning pain of lactic acid eating my muscles was making me wince, but the rhythm was comforting and soon my legs found their strength. I always knew I could rely on them. They were like a clunky old steam engine, its pistons chugging back to life.

I focused on my breathing, forcing myself to inhale deeply. I would blow the valves open again and tell myself to trust that the mask was feeding me life-giving oxygen.

There were three valves on the mask: one to let in pure oxygen from the tank on my back, another valve that let in ambient air, and a third for me to breathe out through. Oxygen is toxic on its own, so with each breath the first two valves would open and the pure oxygen would mix with the air around me, and I would then expel it through the final valve.

With my footsteps steady and my breathing falling into line, I could deal with the aches and pains elsewhere. The oxygen canister digging into my neck? I shuffled my pack sideways. The blisters on my feet and hip bones? Nothing I could do about those now. I forced myself to focus on something else to try and forget about the pain. I had done this many times, and now I was doing it when it really mattered.

Out of the corner of my eye I could see down the Khumbu Valley to Pangboche, and I thought of the girl I was a month ago, when I stood on that chilly morning with a cup of tea and looked up in awe at the might of Everest, unable to imagine myself battling my way through the death zone, realising that nobody down there would be able to hear my screams. Thinking about that girl now brought a smile to the corners of my lips. The pain of my blisters subsided for a moment. I wasn't that girl now. Everest had stripped me down and built me back up into something else. I could deal with these blisters; I could deal with the cold. I could survive in the death zone. I was as feral and as much a part of this mountain as the wind and snow that danced across its flanks. I was hardened and windswept like the rock. I was raw, and yet everything left was everything that counted. *You're climbing Everest,* I said to myself. *You're actually doing it.*

Settled and focused, I drew my attention away from the nagging worry of frostbitten fingers and toes and forced my gaze on to the mountain. Moonlight dappled across the ice and illuminated our intended route. Ahead of us were 850 vertical metres of climbing, but many times more distance in ground covered. First, we would cross the field of scree on the South Col where we'd camped, to reach a sweeping wall of solid ice. We would climb this desolate slope until we reached our rest point at The Balcony at 8,400 metres.

The Balcony signified a break in the route from the lower 'safer' part of the climb, to the more treacherous and risky upper section that led to the summit. From The Balcony, we would turn towards the South Summit at 8,700 metres, and then drop down again to cross a corniced ridge, before facing up to the Hillary Step, a fortress of rock and ice that fiercely guarded the summit. If we could make it over the Hillary Step, then there was nothing between us and the top of the world but a gentle snow slope. That, and the suffocating air at 8,850 metres, where there was only 30 per cent of the oxygen available to us compared to sea level.

None of us knew how long the summit push would take. Some climbers had reached the top in less than six hours from Camp Four; others took more than twelve. Looking up, I could see the studded line of head torches climbing into the night sky, the rigid line betraying the fact that these golden orbs weren't in fact stars. Other climbers were already on their way, battling through their pain and exhaustion, each straining towards the same goal. Joining our place at the back of the line meant we would be climbing at the rate of everyone in front. I took a deep breath and resigned myself to the fact that it was going to be a long night. There was no point in getting angry at the people in front; it wouldn't make a blind bit of difference. We needed to work and move as one.

There was not a breath of wind as we moved silently across the Col. The world was deep in its icy slumber. I felt as if we were walking towards a sleeping giant. I prayed that the mountain wouldn't stir. It looked too peaceful, too serene ... too *inviting*, even. The South East Ridge lay above us, our passageway to the world above. The stars shone overhead as if part of the mountain itself – we weren't climbing towards a summit, we were climbing into the heavens. Taking in the energy around me, I had a strong sense that there was nothing to be afraid of. *What will be will be*, I thought to myself. I kept taking those steps.

We reached the ice face and Lhakpa Wongchu came up next to me – Lhakpa was to be my 'buddy' as we climbed to the summit. Just like scuba divers, we would stay together within our group, and would look out for each other on the climb. I didn't know Lhakpa that well, but I knew that he had climbed Everest multiple times already and was considered one of our strongest Sherpas. Lhakpa was covered from head to toe in his high-altitude gear and looking like an astronaut. I figured I must've looked the same, but in my mind's eye I was just little old me.

'Okay, Didi?' he said through his mask, sounding as though he was shouting into a pillow, and proffered a thumbs-up.

'Yeah,' I said back, 'are you OK?' and I gave a thumbs-up back. We patted each other on the arm; huge mittens meant it was too difficult to try and shake hands. *We're a team*, was what we were trying to say, without actually saying it. Being next to Lhakpa gave me strength.

As we trudged in single file up the face, we fell into the all-consuming silence of our own thoughts. Each climber going through a battle in his or her mind as to why they were carrying on. It suddenly felt like the last eighteen months of my life had gone in the blink of an eye, and now, the endless hours that stretched ahead would go on for ever. I didn't dare to imagine it being over. *Focus on this moment*, I kept telling myself. I felt as if I was both mother and child in my own mind. Sometimes cooing and reassuring myself with steely determination, other times scared and confused, and wanting nothing more than to lie down and sleep.

My entire world was the small orb of light coming from my head torch. All I could see was my mittens, my feet, and the next step in front of me. I kept hoping that when I raised my head and the beam of light lit up the next step, it would be gentle snow and not rock. The pace slowed as each of us struggled to draw enough oxygen into our lungs to keep moving. Three steps at a time turned to one. I saw Rick's head loll forwards over his chest. I knew how he felt, how the exhaustion was making him want to pass out. I knew because I felt exactly the same way.

The desperate gasps to try and get oxygen into my lungs fast enough started to take their toll. I felt like a terrified bird trapped in the clutches of a compressing jaw. At sea level, humans inhale an average of fifteen times per minute. In the death zone, I was taking over sixty breaths a minute, and would have taken more if my lungs could have worked faster. My lungs and my beating heart were at their limit. My intercostal muscles now felt as if they were tearing with every breath, so fatigued were they from days of just trying to breathe.

I had to keep ripping my mask from my face. Firstly, when the claustrophobia of it sucking on to my mouth and nose got too much, and I needed the unencumbered freedom of being able to take a breath without feeling as if I had a jellyfish stuck over my face. Secondly, because the vapour, dribble and snot that were collecting in my mask were freezing around the valves that let air in and out, and when those truly froze I was literally being suffocated. I would have to snap off the icicles that hung from the valves, and sometimes rip off my mittens to poke a finger into the valve and break the ice crust that had been forming. It was a constant cycle that I would have to keep on top of until the sun rose and – with that – the freezing temperatures.

By midnight we had been climbing for three hours and were somewhere in the middle of this vast, icy face, with no idea of how high up or low down we were as we groped into the darkness. As we kicked our boots into the mountain's face, our crampons bounced straight off the bullet-proof ice and rock. It took a delicate balance of force and precision to place each heavy boot with its spiked claws on to a carefully chosen spot – perhaps where the ice had cracked or where another person's crampon had left a small divot.

I was desperate for water, my mouth and throat dry and rasping. I had been ignoring my thirst for hours, but finally forced myself to stop my elephantine rhythm, find some steady footing and stop to take a drink. I unzipped my down suit to grab one of my water bottles, and felt a rush of hot air escape. My down suit had evidently done a good job of trapping my body heat, which I'd just set free into the atmosphere. *Nice one, Bonnie,* I said to myself. I could feel the cold seeping into my ribcage. It was minus 30°C, and the chill in the air was burning my lungs like frozen acid.

I then had to work out how to get the hard plastic Nalgene bottle to my cracking lips, through the mask and wires that surrounded my face, while wearing a pair of down mittens that were akin to boxing gloves. *Sod it,* I thought. I ripped off my mittens – they hung from my wrists by the string I'd attached through my sleeves. I then pulled the oxygen mask upwards, but it got caught over my plastic goggles, which in turn pushed into my eye sockets and scratched across my forehead. *Dammit!* I pulled the mask down below my chin, the straps pulling tightly around the back of my neck. It took all my energy to hold my mask there, keep my head up straight and lift the bottle in my other hand to my mouth. I poured the cool water carefully into my mouth, while my windpipe still opened and closed every second to catch a breath. I spluttered and coughed as some water went down the wrong way. This was way too much effort. I zipped the bottle back into my breast pocket, feeling its weight pulling down the fabric of my down suit on my shoulders. It would be the last sip of water I'd have for nearly ten hours.

My fingers had started to go numb in those few seconds my mittens were off. I still had a base-layer pair of gloves on, but even those were no match for the elements as the cold began to tighten its icy grip. *If they're numb now, what state will they be in in fifteen hours?* The calculations in my brain told me that if my fingers continued to freeze, their flesh would be starved of oxygen and die before I got back to Camp Four. They would become bulbous, bright-red sausages filled with fluids and pus. And then decay until all the dead flesh, bone and sinew fell off. Many mountaineers have part of a finger or a toe missing to frostbite. I gulped and frantically wiggled my fingers and toes, buried under layers of mittens, gloves, socks and 2-kilo boots. I wondered if they were even part of me any more, or what kind of horrific state they would be in when I saw them again.

I noticed that my feet felt like blocks of wood – cumbersome, yet delicate and splintering. I knew that when I finally got to warm them up they would be excruciatingly painful. But, I couldn't think about that right now. I put any thoughts of the future to the back of my mind. I told myself that this was the only world I'd ever known, that *this was it*. There was no future. Only now. To think of a world beyond the darkness and the omnipotent grip it held over our mortality aroused too many feelings. I couldn't have emotions. Emotions demanded attention that I knew I could not give. It was as if I was back on the running track again, aged 12, singing Billie Piper to myself, trying to keep on top of the bubbling anxieties that lay just under the surface as I raced that 1,000 metres. I was in a rhythm and I needed to keep it going for a while yet.

By 2 o'clock in the morning, the impenetrable ice and rock – over which we had scratched and kicked our way up from the South Col – had given way to a football field of deep powder. The Balcony was up ahead, its shadow cutting a jagged outline against the blanket of stars sitting stubbornly against a velvet-black night sky. But to get to it we faced a quagmire of sugary, slushy snow that we all knew meant one step forwards and two steps back.

As my foot punched through the surface crust and I sank up to my knee, I decided I had no choice but to resign myself to the pain. *This is where you decide whether to be a runner, or a very good runner,* my stepdad's voice said in my mind. This wasn't technical climbing, this wasn't even scary climbing. This was just painful climbing. It felt as if I was pulling my feet out of wet concrete. I couldn't bear the thought of looking up. We were tiny specks in a great expanse of white. I didn't want to be faced with how many more thousands of steps like this I would have to take.

As I floundered in the snow, gasping for air and trying to stop myself from ripping off my oxygen mask, I felt a pressure settle on my right shoulder. I awkwardly turned my head to see it was Lhakpa's gloved hand. I turned around and he gave me a thumbs-up again. 'OK, Didi?' he shouted over the hiss of his oxygen. I nodded and said, 'You?' He nodded back, and then his head dropped on to his chest as he gulped air into his lungs. *Sherpas get tired too*, I thought.

Later on, Lhakpa gave my shoulder a squeeze again. To know that someone was there with me warmed my heart. It made me believe that everything was going to be OK. It was the kind of feeling I got when my parents hugged me as a kid. *I'm right here.* I knew he was there, of course, but that act of thoughtfulness spoke a thousand words. Going above and beyond in this instance wasn't a grand gesture, but the effort it took reminded me that I wasn't alone, and that was the most wonderful feeling in the world.

Later, Lhakpa patted my arm again, this time trying to get my attention. He was pointing down the mountain – and there I saw beneath us flashes of green and yellow light. It was an electrical storm raging in a valley a few thousand metres below us. *We're not supposed to be up here*, I thought. We were in the world of the gods.

The saying goes that the darkest hour comes before dawn, and that was definitely true as we headed towards The Balcony at 8,400 metres. By 5 a.m., the insidious cold had truly taken its grip. I saw Rick and Tom in front of me, both almost bent double as they tried to hug the last remnants of warmth into their core. It felt as if we were in the darkest depths of the mountain, almost sinking into it as the snow rose above our knees with each step. As I tore my foot out of the snow again and collapsed forwards, I realised that I no longer had the strength to lift my other leg. I no longer had the strength to do anything, and I went to sleep.

I woke up a few seconds later still standing, my senses suddenly sharpened. *What the …?* I had dreamt I was in *Harry Potter* – not the *Harry Potter* films but the *Harry Potter* of my mind from the books I'd read as a kid. It was a mishmashed jumbled brain-fart of the Gryffindor common room, Harry's glasses and Hagrid's beard. It took me a moment to realise that I was on a mountain – on Everest, to be precise – and I was heading to the top of the world. I shook my head, viscerally aware of where I was, and managed to lift my foot off the ground and take another step. As my foot sank downwards again, I looked up to see how far we had to go before we reached The Balcony.

I could see the flattened ledge only moments away. I could make out silhouettes of climbers who'd already made it. I saw the plastic tables and chairs and the parasols and promised myself that once I reached the café I would get an ice cream.

I blinked, *what?* The parasols and plastic furniture had gone. *Café? There's no café!* I shook my head and tried to talk myself awake. *Come on, focus.* I took a deep breath and drew as much air as I could into my lungs. I could be hallucinating because I was tired, or I could be hallucinating because I was hypoxic.

Hypoxia means oxygen starvation, and in climbing vernacular relates to the brain specifically. We say people are hypoxic when they're not thinking straight, and in that moment as I swayed awake, I knew that something was up. I shouted to Lhakpa. 'Lhakpa, I think my Os are finished.' He staggered up next to me and roughly grabbed my regulator, which had two dials – one to show how much oxygen was left in the canister, and the other showing the flow rate. Average flow rate in the death zone was between 2.5 to 4 litres per minute; the higher the flow rate, the faster the canister would empty.

Lhakpa had been adjusting my regulator all night, sometimes without me even noticing. When I moved quickly he turned it down slightly, and when I started to slow he turned it up, all while managing his own regulator too. His experience of reaching the summit a previous three times meant he was pretty confident about his ability to judge our progress. We had left Camp Four at 9 p.m. the night before, and had been climbing for eight hours. Even on a low flow rate, my canister would have been out by now. We planned to change our oxygen canisters over once we reached The Balcony, and it seemed as though Lhakpa had timed it perfectly.

Lhakpa pretty much dragged me forwards on to the flattened area of The Balcony and pulled the near-empty canister out of my rucksack. He grabbed another two canisters from the stockpile that he and our other Sherpa teammates had stashed at The Balcony a few days before and spun my regulator on to the fresh canister. I heard the hiss as the regulator pierced into the canister, oxygen spilling out into the near vacuum of the death zone. Within moments, I felt my hazy consciousness clearing.

Energised by the sudden rush of oxygen, I felt clarity as to where I was. Looking up from The Balcony, I could now

Rice Terraces on the route to Arughat – the start of our trek to Mount Manaslu base camp.

Rob Casserley, Val Pitkethly and Mel Proudlock at Camp One on Mount Manaslu.

Camp One on Mount Manaslu. I took all of my photos from this expedition on a disposable camera from Boots. Disposables don't freeze and break at altitude, unlike their more expensive counterparts.

On the false summit of Mount Manaslu with Rob, a great support and friend.

© Emma Jack

The Everest team, from left to right: Alma, Rick, Lynette, David, me, Tom, Lewis and Mick.

Lhakpa Wongchu Sherpa, who helped me on the descent from the summit of Everest. We subsequently climbed Ama Dablam and Lhotse together.

Kenton Cool and I in the Western Cwm the day after reaching the summit of Everest.

Living the high life: heating snow for water with some of the greatest
views on Earth just beyond the tent porch.

On the summit of Mount Everest on the 17th May 2010. I bought the flag for 60p from a shop in Windsor. The flag was 80p but I didn't have enough money. When I told the shopkeeper where I was hoping to take it, he let me off the extra 20p.

Climbing the grey tower of Ama Dablam.

Mount Lhotse, 8,516m. Taken from Camp One on Everest.

On the summit of Lhotse, 26th May 2012.
Myself, Bob Jen and Young Lhakpa.

With my partner in crime Adrian, on a rock climbing holiday in Thailand.

Jumping for joy at Camp after reaching the summit of Ama Dablam.

see the white peak of the South Summit and, beyond that, the rocky fortress of the Hillary Step. The true summit was somewhere in the distance; I couldn't think about that just yet. The next few hours were laid out before me, and it would take all my strength just to make it through.

Lhakpa grabbed my arm and pointed over to my right, down into Tibet. I hadn't seen Tibet until this moment, as the bulk of Everest had always shielded it from view. Now, climbing up the South East Ridge, we were straddling the border between the two countries – Nepal dropping for thousands of metres to our left, and Tibet dropping for thousands of metres to our right. I looked out across the carpet of mountains that stretched for miles all around us. Glaciers and dusty plateaus interspersed with formidable peaks, many of them probably never climbed. The view went uninterrupted until it fell off the edge of the Earth.

And then I saw it. The one thing I'd come to see. The thing that had lit the fire in my heart the first moment I had heard about it in that lecture nearly two years before. It was the thing I had dreamed about in my bedroom and that had kept me going when I was desperate to give up on making those stupid sponsorship cold calls. It was the thing that I wanted to break free of my life for, leaving behind my family and loved ones and risking my life climbing the world's highest mountain to see. It was the curvature of the Earth, and it was illuminated by the fiery orange glow of sunrise.

I fell to my knees and burst into tears. Lhakpa crouched next to me and gave me another gentle pat on the shoulder. Rick and Tom were standing close by and I could hear them exclaiming 'Wow' and pointing at the view. A hush came over our group as we became bathed in that beautiful golden light. Everyone turned their faces towards the sunrise and felt the warmth of its rays on their cheeks. I looked at my mittened hands and could feel my fingers thawing out, life coming back to them.

Moments later the sun burst over the horizon and flooded the valleys of Tibet with glorious pink and orange light. The rays washed over us climbers as we stood or sat just below the top of the world. I watched as the snow around my feet turned pink. Looking down, I could now clearly see the mountains beneath me – the knife-edge summit of Lhotse and the perfect pyramid of Makalu dominated the vista. We had craned our necks to look up at Lhotse when we were on our walk into Base Camp, feeling so small compared to these mighty giants. And yet now we were looking down on these exact same peaks. Still little ants, still just as vulnerable as we were all those weeks ago, but somehow we'd survived and battled on. We had kept on taking those smallest of steps, until those mountains were looking up to us.

It's amazing what humans can do when we put our minds to something, I thought. Nothing had got us this high, except our will to go on, our refusal to give up. Nothing had put us within striking distance of the summit by chance – we'd had to consciously make every decision to keep going along the way. We had had to choose time and time again to not give up, to keep hanging in there. We had made millions of decisions over the course of the expedition to keep going, because giving up was always a question that lingered in our minds with almost every step.

I couldn't fathom how the neurones in my brain had willed my little body to this point on planet Earth. Our minds are the most powerful tools that we have. In the past, mine had willed me to do destructive and dangerous things to myself, but now – now it had put me almost on top of the world. Ultimately, I had made a choice to follow my thoughts in both those instances, living with the consequences of my actions. I was so glad that at some point I had made the choice to listen to the voices that said 'Don't give up' rather than the ones that told me I should.

After a few moments there on The Balcony, we dusted ourselves down and faced up to the final challenge: the climb to the South Summit and the Hillary Step. After more than twenty hours without sleep, I was about to face the biggest physical challenge of my life.

CHAPTER 12

The soul-warming relief of making it through the longest night of my life was quickly replaced with the realisation that we still had so much more to do.

As I stepped away from The Balcony and on to the knife-edge that is the South East Ridge, I cast my mind back to the girl who only one day ago had looked up from Camp Three at 7,100 metres and wondered how on earth she'd ever make it through. It didn't seem like only yesterday. That moment felt like a lifetime ago. So much had happened, and it still wasn't over.

Still, we had made it through the longest night of our lives, survived the deadly temperatures and somehow pushed on. There were so many times during that night when I thought that my only option was to give up, because there was surely no way in hell I would be able to string together enough of these lung-busting, heart-bursting, muscle-tearing steps ... but I had. I had managed to string together every single one, and now I was going to need to string together more. My energy was completely depleted, but I had to find the strength from somewhere to keep going.

By this point, the hiss of my oxygen mask and the awkward push and pull of the valves opening and closing had become normal, and not something that kept making me think I was being choked to death. The aching in my feet had become dulled; I realised that it was only when I thought *blister* in my mind that my blisters actually hurt. My heart and lungs, the bird fluttering in the cage, were now weakened and shallow, but they too had given over to the mountain. With a heavy acceptance, I lifted my leg and, like an elephant, stomped it back down on the ground. I took ten rhythmic breaths and then lifted my other leg. *One step at a time.* I had trusted the process so far. I just had to give myself over to it. The process *was* my strength. I had no physical energy left, no fat reserves nor calories from food, no rest from sleep or hydration from water. All I had was the promise to myself that if I kept taking the little steps, eventually I'd get to where I had for so long wanted to be.

Looking ahead, I knew that this was the last 10 per cent. It was a glorious morning, and blue skies shone to my right, the cloak of darkness and stars hung on my left. Night and day sliced in half by the icy ridge in front of me. Everest separating my past from my future. I took another step. We were so close now.

The gradient steepened sharply, and suddenly we were faced with a near vertical wall of rock below the South Summit. I scoured my mind for reference to this climb in all the books and accounts I'd read in the past, but I couldn't recall any mention of it. I later found out that it had been a particularly dry year on Everest, and this had meant that, for us, a climb that would normally be a steep line of snow steps was now an exposed slab of rock.

I attached my jumar to the fixed line that a Sherpa had no doubt fixed a few days previously, thanking him for the ease with which I could then step up on to the rock and start heaving myself towards the South Summit. A few tugs later, and I was slumped forwards on the rope, completely exhausted. 'Come on, Didi,' Lhakpa shouted up to me. He was always keeping his mind on our oxygen levels. I heaved in a huge gulp of air and slid my jumar up the line again, my arm outstretched above my head. I then pushed my foot down against the rock and pulled myself up level with my hand again. Every muscle in my body had to push and pull at the right moment. The level of lactic acid building in every fibre within me was blinding me with pain. But somehow, I shoved the jumar upwards one last time, and stepped on to gentler ground.

In a near heap on the floor, two boots stepped into my vision. It was Kenton. He had made it to the summit and was on his way back down again. 'Be safe OK?' he said, and gave me a hug. I nodded, but I'm not sure if I had the energy to say anything more than 'Wehey!' which I think meant 'Well done' and 'Hello'.

With Kenton on his way down, it was just myself, Lhakpa, Tom, Rick, Jabu and Young Lhakpa now in our team. Henry was waiting by the radio at Base Camp, and Rob Casserley was somewhere ahead. I staggered up on to the South Summit and took in the view of the Hillary Step as it rose majestically above me, snaking its way to the true summit. A band of cloud blew up from Tibet and shrouded us in white for a moment. I felt wet vapour on my cheek and the breeze in my hair as it passed. I hoped that the weather would hold. I knew that the monsoon was on its way in only a few days' time.

I felt someone tapping my leg and I turned round to see

Anita, one of Henry's team members. She was sitting on the floor, Rob next to her speaking to a Sherpa. She gave me a thumbs-up and pointed towards the summit. I knew what she was trying to say: *It's just up there!* I nodded my head and grabbed her mittened hand. *We're so close now.* The excitement was starting to build.

Crossing the corniced ridge from the South Summit to the start of the Hillary Step, I passed another climber who I'd come to know on the mountain: Manuel from Argentina. He had reached the summit and was now on his way back to the warmth and relative safety of Camp Four, but he stopped to greet me. He put his hands on my shoulders and I saw into his piercing blue eyes – they were watery and stung with emotion. 'So beautiful,' he said. 'So beautiful. Enjoy it, Bonita.' I nodded and felt my bottom lip wobble. I was so happy for him, I could see how much it meant for Manuel to see the summit of Everest, a dream he'd had since being a climber as a boy. I was starting to feel adrenaline surge through my body, but I couldn't allow myself yet to believe I would make it to the top. *Anything can go wrong*, I reminded myself.

With that, I grasped the fixed lines at the bottom of the Hillary Step and made the first dangerous move on to the rock from the snowy path where I'd just been standing. I skated my legs as my crampons slipped on glassy rock, desperately trying to catch some friction and find my footing. Lhakpa, as always, was right behind me. I saw the alarm in his eyes as I skirted about, trying to find my balance.

We carried on climbing: at one point we had to make our way round a huge boulder that was blocking the middle of our intended route. The only way around it was to traverse out to the left, with thousands of metres of air below as the mountain dropped into Nepal. As I gingerly stepped my foot out over the abyss and felt around for something to step on to on the other side of the boulder, I realised my pack was pulling me into space. There wasn't much I could do about it – both my hands were gripped tightly to rope and rock, my left foot was out of sight, pressed down hopefully on to something solid, and I had to push off my right foot and step up on to that left leg. If I let go, I would be spat off the mountain and my weight would shock-load the fixed line, tearing it from its anchor and probably pulling down Lhakpa and Rick and Tom with me. No, I couldn't do anything about my rucksack threatening to slide over my head. *I just have to get on with it,* I told myself, and with that thought I wondered with an odd sense of detachment why I wasn't more scared. As I surveyed the sheer drop beneath me, and the breeze whipping the fabric under my butt, I figured that this was a pretty terrifying situation to be in, and yet I felt nothing. *It must be the altitude,* I figured. My brain was not thinking straight.

I heaved myself up the last few sections of rock on the Hillary Step, often entrusting my life to ropes that I couldn't know were safe to tie my washing on to, let alone my whole body weight. Lhakpa guided me, pointing to the rope he thought best to use, and slowly we edged our way up through tight chimneys and blank open faces, up ledge by ledge, pieces of rock sometimes crumbling in our hands, or a lump of packed snow beneath our feet giving way; in those sudden moments, we would desperately grab for something safe to cling on to. Every time I was startled, though, I felt the sensation of fear with a weird detachment – it was as though, even if Lhakpa were to start sawing my arm off – I would be able to watch him and think, 'I should be scared', without actually feeling anything.

I could barely see my feet as I tried to place my cumbersome boots on to the tiny footholds in the rock. My oxygen mask blocked out most of my vision of the ground directly beneath me. My mittens were useless bags of fluff that meant I couldn't grip anything, except the fixed lines and my jumar. I knew it was dangerous to not keep more points of contact with the rock, but I was aware of the clock ticking and just needing to get up this bloody rock step as fast as we could.

I scraped around with my feet until they locked on to something solid, trusted that my foot placements would hold, as I couldn't see them because of my oxygen mask, and pushed down on each bent leg, standing up to then grab a section of rope a little higher. Small steps, I kept repeating to myself. I tried not to look around too much – I was a red flag fluttering in the wind, nothing but air all around me, a tiny speck clinging to the most exposed part of the climb to the summit.

Finally, I hauled myself over the last ledge and rolled on to the snow. It was done. We had climbed the Hillary Step. It occurred to me that soon we would have to reverse all those moves to get back down it again, but I pushed that horror to the back of my mind. *Focus*, I told myself.

Lhakpa was right next to me again; he patted me on the back and said, 'Let's go, Didi,' and I knew what he meant: '*Let's go to the summit.*'

Through the swirling clouds that were travelling across the mountain, I could see the silhouettes of my teammates a few metres ahead. Beyond them, a trace of white in the white mist, I could see the summit. It was all at once right there in front of me, as if it had always been there, facing me with a total nonchalance and yet asking, 'What took you so long?'

That last stretch took longer than I could ever have imagined. My body was doing its best to move, but each step took at least five breaths. I was covering about seven metres a minute. Lhakpa, my guardian angel, hovered at my shoulder, despite how easy it would have been for him to race to the summit from there.

As we got closer, I could see the prayer flags that other Sherpas had left on the summit fluttering in the wind, and snowflakes that were by that point falling in flurries through the mist. I let out a noise, I'm not sure what noise it was – it was like a groan from somewhere within, an exclamation – as though I had been holding my breath for the last two years and had finally allowed myself to exhale. It was the moment when I realised I was going to make it.

As I took those last few steps to the summit, I could imagine the path of millions of steps stretching out behind me, not just on the mountain, but on the whole journey from that night in the lecture theatre at the RGS. I couldn't believe that somehow I'd managed to not give up. After all, each step had been followed with the choice of whether to give up, or to take another, and, somehow, I had managed to string together every single one, from learning to climb, to phoning up Capital FM, to crossing those ladders in the icefall and making it through summit night.

I give up at everything, I thought, but somehow not at this.

I wondered how on earth I was still standing after so many millions of these tiny steps: where had the energy and strength come from? I did not know. All I knew was, I had kept digging, and somehow I had always found strength. Often in places I didn't know it could exist.

I had drawn strength from my past, and from knowing how far I'd come. I had drawn strength from my teammates and – especially on the last climb – from Lhakpa. I had drawn strength from the mountains themselves, and from the gratitude that came with knowing how lucky I was to be in their company.

I had drawn strength from the thought that I could make my family proud. I had drawn strength from wanting to prove others wrong. I had drawn strength from my favourite songs, and quotes and stories. I had drawn strength from my heroes from the past – Hillary, Tenzing Norgay and Shackleton. I drew strength from knowing that – one day in the future – I would look back on this and be glad I didn't give up. I drew strength from promising myself that it was just *one more step*. And finally, I had drawn strength from the struggle itself, knowing that I could *lean in* to the fear and the pain, and get through seemingly impossible moments.

I had drawn strength from all of those places and many more, and perhaps it had taken me to face up to the world's highest mountain to see just how much strength I really had, and how lucky I was to be able to draw upon so much.

As I took that final step, I didn't believe I was about to 'conquer' Mount Everest. No human can ever conquer nature. Everest was as unconquerable as the rising sun and the spin of the galaxies. I felt that all I did was conquer the next step.

I cried gently into my mask, tears falling down frozen cheeks. I was standing on top of the world.

CHAPTER 13

I wish I could write about how beautiful the view from the top of the world was; how I stood and surveyed the Kingdom of Tibet beneath my feet, and marvelled at the curvature of the Earth as if I was looking down on our planet from space. I wish I could write how I got to the top and punched the air, how I felt 'on top of the world' and full of jubilation.

But I can't.

In truth, I stood for those first few moments – in the middle of a big cloud – with a dulled sense of detachment. Specks of snow and a wet blanket of mist settled on my down suit. Wind blustered across my face, scouring the gaps of skin between my goggles and oxygen mask. Cloud continuously rose up from Tibet and over the summit, tumbling over it into Nepal.

The only sound was that of prayer flags fluttering in the breeze. The hallowed chill and white aura that surrounded us gave way to the occasional ghostly whisper as the wind whistled past. I couldn't see a thing, but I didn't need a view to tell me that I was standing on sacred ground. I could *feel* it. I was struck with awe and humbled by the beckoning silence. I didn't feel part of planet Earth any more. This was a place where man and God could reach out and touch.

And yet, despite the frisson in the air, all around me other climbers moved in slow motion, doing the most mundane things – checking oxygen regulators, radioing down to Base Camp, gulping down a precious few mouthfuls of water and taking out flags of their home countries or sponsors. It seemed like any other moment, nothing special: people getting on with the task at hand.

My hypoxic brain mused that this was exactly what it was like whenever I climbed in North Wales. Thick cloud, no views, people milling about. Nothing profound and enlightening. *Just like Mount Snowdon*, I thought.

A friend of mine, Roger, said that when he reached the summit of Everest in 2012, he queued in line behind a group of climbers believing he was at a bus stop waiting to get on the bus. I guess my oxygen-starved brain wasn't hallucinating quite so badly in that moment, but putting the summit of Everest in the same box as Mount Snowdon in Wales probably showed the extent to which I was unable to think straight.

Then, a gap in the clouds appeared, and for a second I could spy the blue sky beyond – it looked like a beautiful day. I could see the haze on the horizon, and the Earth curving in all directions. I really wasn't on Mount Snowdon. It was 10 a.m. on 17 May 2010, and I was standing on the summit of Mount Everest.

Then came the relief. A tidal wave of it, washing over me. It flooded through my veins like a drug and brought me to my knees. I crashed to the floor, and rubbed my hands in the snow, gathering the precious ice crystals in the creases of my mittens – they sparkled like fairy dust.

For a moment, I forgot the pain and the cold and the

fear. I wanted to laugh from the relief. It was better than jubilation. Better than any feeling I had ever felt. It was the realisation that – after all the risk and worry and not knowing – I was right where I was always supposed to be. I was right to trust my instincts. Somehow they had known all that time ago that this was where I would end up.

I got up and staggered forward another few steps, past other climbers who were sitting down or hunched over their packs, and I reached out my hand and rested it on the crest of the summit. I wouldn't go any higher. It was a mark of respect. A 'thank you' to the mountain for letting me crawl up its flanks and spend these precious few moments at its peak. Leaving those last few centimetres will always mean that my and Everest's story remains unending.

I turned around to see Lhakpa sitting down, cradling his rucksack and taking a few moments for himself. It was his fourth summit of Everest. He was twenty-two years old, like me, and fast becoming a rising star in his community in Pangboche village. I staggered over and knelt down next to him. He put his arm around my shoulder and shook me as if to say 'We've done it.'

We sat in a tangle of wires, buried beneath our layers of kit, and just hugged. I couldn't speak. It was as if my brain was in sensory overload, trying to deal with a million thoughts all at once, and so of course I couldn't think anything coherent at all. I wish I could have said something profound or momentous to Lhakpa, but all I could manage was a snotty 'Thank you' as I buried my head in his shoulder.

Lhakpa radioed down to Henry and Kami at Base Camp. I watched him shout Nepalese into the freezing lump of scuffed metal, hearing the crackle of Kami's voice cut through the air of the summit. It didn't occur to me to speak to Henry myself, which I've always regretted. I felt so thankful to him, and must have thought that somehow he knew that without hearing my voice.

When I looked up, I caught sight of Rick and Tom a few steps away. Tom was taking a photo of Rick with a T-shirt he was holding proudly across his chest. It was emblazoned with the words 'Living The Dream Boys' in Rick's handwritten capital letters. I don't know why, but that bloody T-shirt got the most visceral reaction of all. I sobbed and spluttered and my whole body shook. I laughed and cried. I was so happy and proud of him.

I had watched and been a part of his and Tom's journey and knew intimately why they were here. We had spent nights in high camps together talking about our loved ones back home, and why we had chosen to leave them behind and risk our lives climbing this mountain. I had known them both as Rick and Tom, doctor and pilot from the United States, and now I knew them as Rick and Tom, Everest summiteers. They would never be the same again, and I felt proud to witness a moment that I knew they so deserved.

And I was there too with them. *I'm an Everest summiteer,* I had to tell myself. I still couldn't believe it. I looked at my team in awe at what they'd just achieved, but I didn't see myself in the same light. I knew that I would never have made it here without them, or our incredible Sherpas. I wouldn't have had a hope in hell alone on a mountain like Everest. But, together, we somehow got to the top. We hadn't started out as a team – we were a group of strangers when we met in Kathmandu, but we grew together as we climbed.

I saw Rick wipe a tear from behind his goggles. I knew how close he was to his sons, and how much he had missed them. This summit was for them. I thought about my family too. They were five and a half miles below me, and thousands of miles across the other side of the planet. It would have been around 6 a.m. in England. Little did I know that my parents had lain awake all night in anguish, worrying about what their daughter might be going through in that moment; barely able to imagine me battling my way through a world so alien and far away. Not knowing as the seconds passed whether I had just taken my last breath.

As I sat on the summit, my bum getting cold, I believed my parents were soundly asleep in bed – again, my oxygen-starved brain was thinking the complete opposite of what had actually happened, but in that moment I was quite jealous of them. I hadn't thought of them at all in the last thirteen hours, and I assumed they had gone about their day as usual, not thinking much about me. *If only I had known the truth*. I wished I could have called them, but Kenton was the only person that I knew had a satellite phone, and he was back at Camp Four. I would have loved to have been able to transport them here next to me, so we could share this moment together. I knew that they were going to be so proud.

Lhakpa was suddenly holding a mobile phone out towards me. 'Picture please, Didi.' I slowly pushed myself on to my feet, wobbling like a drunk, and took the phone. It was a camera-phone and I remember being slightly surprised that Lhakpa had a better phone than I did. I snapped a grainy photo of him holding a picture of Lama

Geshe, a famous Bhuddist teacher who lived in Pangboche village, where Lhakpa was from. He then pulled out a picture of his family, and I cursed myself again for not thinking to bring a picture of my own family to the top of the world.

Then, Lhakpa helped me with the mammoth task of unfurling five huge flags that my sponsor VocaLink had given me to take to the summit. I was so worried that one would break free from my grasp and blow away that I took my gloves off.

Within fifteen minutes, our little team was packing up and getting ready to leave again. After the rush of relief and the tears of pride for my teammates, I felt a sense of foreboding start to weigh on my chest and raise my heart rate back up again.

Now we have to get back down.

No helicopter or plane could pick us up from this height. The only way off this mountain was to turn around and retrace our footsteps, returning just as we'd come. Risking our lives on all the same death-defying landmarks – climbing down the Hillary Step and the Lhotse face, crossing the ladders in the icefall and walking underneath the avalanche-prone flanks of Nuptse.

Please let us get off this mountain alive, I prayed as I fastened my rucksack around my waist. This was it, the final challenge. It would take us another three days to get back down. Only once we were back at the safety of Base Camp could we truly celebrate. Lhakpa and I took one last look at the summit, and then we turned and began our journey home. All in, we spent a little over 15 minutes on the top of the world. Two years of effort for just 15 minutes.

From Base Camp, Henry watched the weather up high with a sense of foreboding. The weather reports had stated that we had a clear window on the night of 16 May, but that conditions would deteriorate as the 17th wore on. It was 10 o'clock in the morning, and it seemed that the summit was already smothered with thick cloud and snowfall. But, as long as the winds didn't pick up, Henry couldn't see a reason to get too worried – not yet, anyway.

'Now get down safely,' he had said to us over the radio. 'No mistakes.'

CHAPTER 14

Lhakpa and I were making good time as we tramped away from the summit, taking great leaps as steps, letting gravity pull us downwards. I felt a sudden surge of energy. I could see Base Camp in my mind, and to me that represented everything: home, my family, my future. I knew with every step that I was getting closer and, as we descended, I was able to draw in more oxygen from the atmosphere with every breath.

We passed climber after climber slumped at the side of the route, barely moving. I looked at them in horror. *What are they doing?* I wondered. Why anyone would want to rest when home was so close was beyond me. They looked like dead bodies. They would *be* dead bodies if they didn't get moving, I thought.

I felt proud of Lhakpa and myself as we bounded past. It seemed as though we were going to make it back to Camp Four in good time. If it was the last 10 per cent that got a person to the summit of Mount Everest, then this was the last 1 per cent – the final push that you really had to dig deep for.

I knew how hard descents could be. I had floundered across the crevasse field between Camps Two and Three on Mount Manaslu, completely exhausted until Mel, a guy from our larger team, had stopped and helped me back to camp. By the time we'd arrived – after dark, and completely exhausted from the summit push – I was a mess, my body and mind completely overwhelmed by what I'd just put them through.

I was not going to let that happen this time, I thought. And, with that, I picked up one of the ropes anchored into the ice by my feet, clipped in my safety karabiner and wrapped it around my arms. Then I stepped off the summit slope and on to the near-vertical rock wall of the Hillary Step.

As I took that step down on to the face, I expected to feel the rope come tight behind me as I pulled my weight on to it. That moment never came. The rope was caught around a jagged piece of rock, and as I jumped over the edge, I had flicked the rope off the point on which it was caught, meaning that loads of rope slack was now suspended in the air, and I was falling, the loose rope wrapped around my body.

I lost my footing and tumbled sideways down the Hillary Step. A split second later the rope came tight and the shock-load spun me around, elbows, knees and face hitting and grazing against the rock as the rope unwound itself. I swung like a pendulum, and slammed into the rock face.

For a moment I hung there in a daze, gulping for air. It had all happened before anyone had been able to stop it. I slid down the rest of the rope and touched the toes of my boots on to the ledge below. I was OK. It was just a small slip. *Concentrate more*, I scolded myself. *The descent is where people die.*

Lhakpa zipped down the rope behind me. 'Are you OK?'

'Yeah …' I gasped as I tried to calm the adrenaline

surging through my body. With that, he stepped around me, and signalled for us to keep going.

I knew something was wrong as we stepped off the final rocky section of the Hillary Step and began to walk across the traverse that would take us to the bottom of the South Summit. All we had to do was climb a few metres to the top of the South Summit, and then it was downhill all the way back to Camp Four. This short traverse was where the mountain guide Rob Hall had died in 1996. He had been too exhausted and suffering from hypoxia to muster the strength to climb those last few metres. And now I found myself slumped in the exact same spot, unable to move as excruciating pain seared from my shoulder, up my neck and into the back of my head.

My vision was blinded by the throbbing pain going through the back of my neck, and my left arm hung limp at my side. Lhakpa stood staring at me, not sure what to do. I wasn't sure what to do either. All I could think was *keep moving,* so I tried to take another step. As my heavy boot hit the ground, a shock wave went up my spine and exploded in my upper back. I yelped out, 'Lhakpa, something's up.' I didn't know what. I was totally blind-sided.

We slumped ourselves against the exposed rock of the ridge to our left, looking towards the South Summit. It suddenly loomed over me as if it was hundreds of metres high. I couldn't lift my left arm. Every time I tried, I got shooting pains from my shoulder to my neck and head.

We watched as hordes of climbers began to pass us, one after another, on their way down from the summit. These were the people we had overtaken not long ago. Now, they had risen like ghosts from their graves to make their way back down to Camp Four.

The fog was so thick that an early dusk had set over the mountain. I could only see silhouettes through the mist, one appearing after another, until finally no more people appeared. The last climber passed me and I found myself blurting out, 'Have you got any painkillers?' Fortunately the figure stopped and took off his rucksack, dug out some paracetamol and proffered them. I ripped off my mitten and he dropped two little white pills on to my palm.

As I lifted my oxygen mask and tried to put the pills in my mouth with the same hand, my left arm still hanging limp beside me, my mitten slipped off my lap and skidded away into thin air. It disappeared in an instant, swallowed by the thick, swirling cloud. 'NO!' I shouted as it tumbled away.

'Jeez!' the climber with the drugs said. We all watched in disbelief as the white ocean swirled menacingly beneath us.

The climber shook his shoulders at me and said, 'Just get yourself over the South Summit, it's all downhill from there,' in his American drawl. There wasn't much else he could do, and he left. He was the last one. Now, it was just Lhakpa and me, two tiny dots on the great expanse of Everest's summit ridge.

Clutching my mitten-less hand into my chest, I squeezed my eyes shut and begged, *Please let this be a nightmare.* Within the space of an hour, we had gone from racing back to Camp Four to now facing up to the fact that we were starring in our own disaster movie. I still had my base-layer glove on, but it was only a thin layer of wool, and with every minute passing the temperature was dropping. The death zone was tightening its insidious grip over us and, that night, it looked as though it would claim two new victims.

Lhakpa didn't say anything as I cried into my mask. He stood over me, completely at a loss as to what to say. 'Come on, Didi,' he tried, and patted my arm. 'I can't,' I said, wincing from the shooting pains going through my neck from where he'd just touched me.

Lhakpa stepped away and grabbed the radio from his chest pocket. He spoke hurriedly in his language. I wished I understood what he was saying. I gazed at my thinly gloved hand. *How long until I get frostbite?* I thought. I didn't wonder that with a sense of panic, more just with the sorry realisation that *this was it; this is how the story ends*. I was going to get frostbite and probably freeze to death. I needed to tell Lhakpa to save himself.

'Lhakpa just go!' I shouted over to him, interrupting him as he talked frantically down the radio. He stepped back over to me and said, 'Didi, we *have to move*.'

'I can't,' I yelped back.

'If we don't move, we die here!'

I looked into Lhakpa's eyes and I could see pure desperation. He was scared for his life. I felt sick to my stomach. It gave me the shock I needed. Suddenly, I had enough clarity to murmur to myself: *Screw the pain.*

I pushed myself off the wall of rock, and winced with every slight movement as electric shocks ripped through my left side.

With what felt like the mightiest effort, I groped for the fixed lines hanging down from the South Summit and stabbed my feet into the rock, standing up on each foothold and crying out in pain. I felt as if a laser was burning streaks of flesh off the back of my neck, searing into my brain and burning a hole through my forehead.

I collapsed into the snow on the South Summit, retching with the nausea of lactic acid, draining my last reserves. Lhakpa climbed up behind me a few seconds later. We had done it. It was all downhill from here.

Heaving and coughing, and trying to steady my convulsing body, I looked ahead and saw nothing but a great expanse of white surrounding us on all sides, cutting us off from the world below. It was deadly quiet, almost too quiet.

There was not a soul in sight. Everybody had gone. They would be safe in their sleeping bags at Camp Four by now. I felt as though we'd been abandoned; left behind on a school trip. Soon someone would realise we were missing and come back for us, surely? For now, though, Lhakpa and I were on the roof of the world, and we were all alone.

We slid down the snowy ridge from the South Summit in silence, hardly able to distinguish snow and sky – all about us was white. The steep drops either side into Nepal and Tibet were totally hidden by the thick white fog. After a few minutes, a figure came into view ahead on the route. It looked like a boulder, but as we trudged through the snow, we realised it was a human. *Someone else is injured*, I thought.

It was Rick, sitting in the snow, and he wasn't injured. He was waiting for us.

Seeing Rick gave me a surge of energy. I don't think I'd ever been so happy to see someone in my whole life. Rick represented a link to the rest of the world below us. Lhakpa and I weren't alone after all.

'What's happened?' Rick asked as I slid down next to him, wincing as another jolt of pain burned through my body. 'I fell,' was all I could manage to say.

A short conversation later, and it was agreed that Lhakpa would head down to The Balcony and change his oxygen bottle; he would then bring up a fresh canister for Rick and me. Meanwhile, we would hopefully meet him as close to The Balcony as possible.

With that, Lhakpa was enveloped in the mist. I thought we would see him in a few minutes, but it was to be hours before we met again. Suddenly, the world went quiet. It was now just me and Rick. Another guardian angel risking his life to help me down.

Rick and I made it to the exposed rocky slope that we'd encountered with confusion when we headed up to the South Summit. In normal circumstances I would have been able to arm wrap here and walk forwards down the mountain without any problem at all. However, I was now so weakened by the pain in my left side that I didn't trust myself on such steep ground.

Rick pulled the frozen fixed ropes into his belay device and attached it to the front loop on my harness. As he did this, he saw that my right hand wasn't gloved.

'Where's your glove?' he demanded, holding my hand and rubbing it furiously. 'Your hand is frozen.' I hadn't even noticed. 'Here,' he said, pulling off his own mitten and shoving it on to my hand.

'Rick …!' I feebly exclaimed.

'Wear the glove – warm your hand up.'

I wanted to accept the offer. I realised I couldn't feel my fingers at all.

We slipped and crashed our way down the rocky slope, and then finally made our way on to the steep ice slopes above The Balcony. It was taking all of Rick's strength to keep me moving. I was delirious with pain. He kept stopping me and saying, 'You've got to hold it together.' I knew I did, but it seemed as though my body wasn't listening to my mind any more. My legs were jelly, my balance swaying dangerously from side to side. Rick was sure I was going to walk right off the side of the mountain. He took out a nylon sling and attached one end to his harness and one end to mine; that way we were 'shot roped' together, with only a metre between us at all times. 'Walk,' he demanded, and I staggered forwards a few steps before having to stop as the pain in my shoulder and neck threatened to obliterate me.

Why Rick didn't just leave me there, I'll never know. For him, the safety and warmth of Camp Four was only an hour's descent away. At my pace, we would be lucky to make it there alive. Somehow, it was now 5 o'clock in the evening. Twenty hours since we'd left Camp Four.

Finally, Lhakpa's silhouette came into view. It was such a relief to see another human. He brought fresh oxygen, and I remember the rush of cool air flowing into my lungs as the new canister was turned up to the max, pumping my blood full of life-giving energy. If anything was going to keep me moving, it was lots of oxygen.

We made it down to The Balcony, an empty expanse that had been so teeming with life the last time I was there. Lhakpa handed me his radio, and Henry's voice crackled to life. He spoke soothingly, as if he was right there with us. 'Bonita, it's Henry. Don't worry, everything's going to be OK. We've got some Sherpas coming up to help. We're going to get you down. Don't worry. Stay calm. We're right here.'

'Thanks Henry,' I managed to splutter. And then I started to cry. I cried in utter disbelief at the situation. I couldn't believe I was causing so much trouble. One small mistake. One lapse in concentration. What should have been a day when my dreams came true had turned into my worst nightmare. Not a nightmare because I was scared for my own life, but because others were risking theirs.

I was torn between wanting Rick and Lhakpa to just leave me behind, and wanting them desperately to stay and help me. Their presence and solidarity was the only strength I could draw upon.

Finally, Rick and Lhakpa were relieved by the arrival of the rest of our Sherpa team. Rick left his mitten on my hand. I didn't even realise.

The Sherpas had turned around once they'd arrived at Camp Four, and walked back up into the death zone as the sun dropped out of the sky, finding themselves out on its unforgiving slopes for the second night in a row.

When they reached our little group, I was sitting with my legs in front of me, pushing myself down the powder slope that we had floundered in on our way up. The guys figured that this was probably my fastest way down, and they tied a sling to my harness, and short-roped me as I slid down the mountain.

At first, I was yelping in pain as they dragged me down as fast as they dared. I was hitting rock and lumps of ice, thudding my spine and pelvis. After a while, though, I couldn't cry out any more. I had no energy to exclaim at the pain. I couldn't even wince. I shut my eyes and told myself that this was all my fault, and that I deserved every punch and kick.

I opened my eyes sometime later to see the now-familiar blanket of stars above me. It was the middle of the night. We'd been out in the death zone now, in temperatures as low as minus 30°C, for over 24 hours. This truly felt like the only world I'd ever known.

I saw head torches above me, and heard barks of Nepalese through oxygen masks. My entire body was frozen and painfully numb. I wished it all away. I wished I didn't exist. I wanted these men to go to their warm sleeping bags and not be out here with me. I didn't think about my family, or home. I just wanted to not exist.

At 11 o'clock in the evening, 26 hours after I'd left Camp Four, I saw the head torch of Kenton approaching me. I could see orange tents behind him. It was over; we had made it.

The Sherpas passed my near-lifeless body over to Kenton and he ripped open my down suit. Another climber, Greg, was there next to him, and I saw through my blurred vision a needle and syringe in his hand. 'What are you doing?' I tried to protest. It was dexamethasone. I couldn't understand it. I wasn't suffering from altitude sickness; I had fallen down the Hillary Step. But still, what did I know? I wasn't exactly in a position to start arguing with someone who had left their tent in the hope of helping me. He pushed the needle into my arm. I couldn't feel it. I was too numbed from the cold.

Kenton and Victor Saunders, another wonderful British climber who had volunteered to come and help, lifted me to my feet and dragged me over to the tents. I was thrown inside our little cocoon and saw the faces of my teammates Tom and Rick, exhausted and yet wired with panic.

Kenton tore at my boots, pulling off my crampons and casting them aside. He had tears in his eyes. 'Your feet, Bonita ...' was all he could say. He yanked off my boot and my sock slid off with it. Everyone was holding their breath, expecting the horror show of a milky-white foot that meant serious frostbite. Instead of recoiling in horror, their faces sank with relief. My feet were absolutely fine. I had superficial frostbite in the tips of two toes. How my feet had survived after being frozen in the death zone for that long is a miracle.

I can't remember anything more. Sleep engulfed me. I dreamt of Harry Potter and Dumbledore and Platform Nine and Three-Quarters. Thanks to the herculean efforts of my teammates, the death zone, on that night at least, had not managed to claim another victim.

CHAPTER 15

News of my summit had swept down the mountain hours beforehand, and was already starting to make headlines back in the UK. I had become the youngest British woman to climb Everest, taking Tori James's title, at the age of twenty-two. My parents had sat at the office computer scouring the internet for updates until there it was: a story on BBC News confirming that Kenton had made his eighth summit of Everest, and that I had made it shortly after.

They had hoped for more news all day, but none came. They knew that the descent was the most dangerous part. Jubilation slowly began to be replaced by stomach-churning uncertainty. My stepdad paced around the house and my mum went into 'zombie' mode – going through the motions of her day in a haze, all the time thinking: *Why hasn't Bonnie called?*

In the dead of night, my stepdad lay thinking about what might have happened to me when the phone rang. *Who the hell rings at this time?* It was a journalist. 'How do you have our phone number?' my stepdad asked.

'What do you think about your daughter's fall?' the voice interrupted.

'Fall?' Rob repeated.

'Yes, she's fallen on the way down. How do you feel? She might die up there …'

My stepdad told the journalist in some very colourful language to leave them alone and not call again. He put the phone down and turned over to see my mum still sound asleep. Should he wake her? He daren't. He lay staring at the ceiling all night, wondering how the hell he was going to break the news to her in the morning.

What if she's already dead?

CHAPTER 16

Wind battered the tent. The tent poles rattled as fabric fluttered back and forth. Opening my eyes, a greyish world came into vision, all colour dulled. Around me were the cocoons of sleeping bags. Save for the wind whistling outside, there wasn't a sound.

The world was eerily still. *Where am I?*

One of the sleeping bags stirred. I wasn't sure who or what it was, but then I saw the matted, sweat-streaked hair of Rick.

Then it hit me: *We're at Camp Four on Everest.* Memories came flooding back – reaching the summit, my fall, and then the near-deadly descent. My heart soared and crashed in a single moment. We had done it, *but what the hell had happened next?*

I pushed myself up on to my elbows and looked around the tent, just as Kenton sat up and rubbed his eyes. *I'm sure I'm not dreaming; I'm sure this is real.*

'Kenton,' I heard my raspy voice. 'We made it!'

His eyes widened, from half-asleep to wide-awake in less than a second. He spluttered, 'Not yet. We're not down yet. We haven't done it until we get down.'

I recoiled backwards into my sleeping bag; the fear in his eyes burned into mine. I had a sinking feeling in my stomach. He was right. We were still in the death zone,

Base Camp was another day away, and I didn't know if I would be able to walk.

Rick and Tom stirred awake. Bleary eyes were rubbed and chests cleared. They were a sorry-looking sight, now bearing the scars of Everest.

I couldn't help but feel proud that we had gone to the top of the world and back together. But any sense of lightness from knowing that the summit had been reached was put to the back of my mind. We still had a huge task ahead.

An hour later I managed to stagger out of the tent, able to walk unaided, but my neck and shoulder were blinding me with pain.

At the top of the Geneva Spur I held out my hand as a fellow climber emptied a cocktail of drugs into it. I chucked them into my mouth and, from then on, I was in a dream world as I climbed down the steep black rocky spur with the ground rushing towards my feet, mountains moving like water in the background and everything seeming big and small at the same time.

We reached Camp Two that afternoon, and were greeted by the smiling faces of Pasang Temba, the cook, and Kumar, the cook boy. I was aware suddenly of how dreadful we must look – and of the stench of sweat rising off us.

Pasang Temba cooked us a celebratory meal of egg and chips, but I could barely stomach a mouthful. In the mess tent, Rick had finally got a chance to look at his wounds from the night before, and I was horrified to see him grimace as he pulled off his gloves. He had frostbite on four fingers of his hand – the hand that had been left exposed after he'd given his glove to me. At this stage, they were milky-white at the tips with a tinge of yellow bruising.

'War wounds,' Rick half joked. 'They'll be fine,' he said, seeing my horrified face.

'I'm so sorry, man,' I muttered back. I knew he was just trying to make me feel better. I was still so confused about what had happened – *how had this happened?* I looked at Rick's frozen hand and thought, *This is all my fault.* I hung my head on my chest, totally ashamed.

As dusk fell on the mountain for our sixth night since leaving Base Camp, I crawled into my own tent, alone for the first time in three days.

I pulled the sat-phone batteries out of my sports bra. They felt warm from where they'd been next to my heart. I fumbled to get them into the satellite phone I'd borrowed from Kenton, and finally did what I'd been waiting all day to do: call my parents.

The phone seemed to ring for ever. Tears welled up, even though I hadn't heard my mum or dad's voices yet. It was the first time I had allowed myself to think of them since leaving the summit some 33 hours previously.

'Hello?' My mum answered, and before she'd even finished I replied, 'Mum, it's me!' knowing that the two-second delay would confuse her if I waited to speak for too long.

'It's Bonnie, it's Bonnie,' I heard her saying to the rest of the family. 'Are you OK, sweetheart?'

'I'm fine, Mum,' I found myself saying, like all kids do, no matter what we've been through – whether we've just climbed Everest or had a long day at work. 'I'm OK.'

I had planned to tell her that I'd reached the summit

and would be at Base Camp the next day. I wasn't going to mention my fall.

'What happened, darling? We've been so worried about you?' I felt my mum's voice waver as emotion got the better of her. Confused, I asked, 'What do you mean?'

As she told me how my ascent and descent had been dramatised across the national press, I felt the air being punched out of my lungs. As I'd climbed down from Camp Four, my parents had been in turmoil, wondering if I was alive. I'd had no idea of what they had been suffering. My nightmare seemed to be spiralling out of control. I couldn't bear how much pain I had put so many people through.

The connection was worsening, her voice crackling and broken. I promised her that I was OK and that I'd ring again at Base Camp, not sure if she could hear me, and switched off the call. I felt the tent walls closing around me. Tears ran down my cheeks. *What was going on back home?*

The next day we trudged through the icefall under the beating heat of the sun. It had become an alien world – so much had changed. Where there was once ice there were now glacial streams. Ladders had melted into crevasse walls or collapsed altogether in the spring melt. The mountain was shutting down for another year, and we had made it off just in time.

Finally, we staggered into the final icy stretch between the icefall and Base Camp. It was a beautiful crisp day; the sky was a deep blue, the mountain gleamed in brilliant white. The sun bore down on us, and I could smell the sweat rising from my body. *I'll have a wash today*, I thought. I could hear birdsong and I could smell food cooking in the different camps – we were so close. When I took the last step off the mountain, my legs turned to jelly. It was as though my whole body wanted to collapse with the relief of knowing that it had done its job.

I felt so many different emotions – pride that I'd been successful and part of a brilliant team, and joy in knowing that we were all alive and would be able to go home soon. Then there were the feelings of confusion and horror: *How did it all go so wrong?* I was so ashamed.

Our Base Camp crew, Sherpas and other teammates who had arrived before Lhakpa and me were banging pots and pans and cheering as we entered camp. I wanted to rip the pots out of their hands. I didn't deserve this. I shouldn't be celebrating. Looking back, surely our survival was enough of a reason to celebrate, but my emotions were just too raw at the time.

I stopped and took off my backpack. As I went to undo my hip belt, I realised I could get my hands clean through the gap. I took off the straps and, in that moment, I felt the weight of the mountain lift off my shoulders. I looked back up to the Khumbu Icefall – a simmering beast gleaming in the sun – and thought: *I never have to go up there again.* The fog cleared for a second and I smiled. *We're alive.*

I gave Lhakpa a hug and, when we came apart, I could see he felt awkward. I didn't know what to say. I wanted to say 'Thank you for saving my life.' Somehow, the words failed me. I couldn't even look into his eyes.

I looked on as everyone around me sipped beers and laughed and felt the weight of their achievement sink in. I had dreamed of this moment for so long but, now it was here, I watched in detachment, unable to shake the numbing shock of what I'd been through – what I'd put my team through.

That night Bhim made us a cake to celebrate. How he had managed to bake a cake at 5,300 metres without an oven was beyond us. It was oozing with sticky, sugary blue icing and had 'Congratulations Summit 2010' written in red letters. The atmosphere for a moment felt light and celebratory. I sat in silence listening to everyone speak. Hearing the bursts of laughter and the usual banter washing over me, I began to gain a little perspective: we were all alive; we had all had fun; we had all made it to the summit. Whatever else had happened, we had those three things. It seemed as though, to the rest of the team, the harrowing experience of my fall had not dampened the fact that they were now Everest summiteers.

We chinked beers around the table and, one by one, began regaling the others with summit stories. Rick was rightly hailed a hero. He could have gone down to the safety of Camp Four, but he had waited up high in the death zone, the weather closing in, to help a fallen team-mate. There is a saying that goes, 'Mountains are like mirrors – it's only when you're up against them that you find out what you're truly made of.' In this case, the mountains had reflected Rick's true grit. He had seen the top of the world, and then he had dug deeper within himself than anyone could have ever asked. Though, when he spoke, he came across not as a boastful hero but as a humbled and self-effacing man. He didn't want recognition, he just wanted a beer and to get home to his boys.

The next day, I was ready to leave. A helicopter was

coming to pick me up and take me to a hospital in Kathmandu. It was all too fast; I felt that I had come to call Everest Base Camp home. I wasn't ready to say goodbye. I had never felt so content and yet so alive waking up every morning, knowing that I was in the most special place on Earth. And now, suddenly, after dreaming about this place for so long, it was over.

I stood outside my tent, my bags piled up next to me, and I felt so much emotion rising in my chest. The mountains looked so beautiful and serene, so unaffected by the horrors of that night. I felt as though I was being dragged down into that dark well again, but the mountains were still there, telling me I was always welcome. As I climbed into a helicopter ready to take me to hospital in Kathmandu, I took one last look at the majestic amphitheatre around me, breathed in the thin mountain air, and waved goodbye to the Sherpas.

A group of them had come to see me off and, as we were about to take off, they rushed forward and reached out their hands. Lhakpa Wongchu, Namgel, Thundu, Hemanta and Bhim. I reached out and touched the tips of their fingers. One last moment. 'Bye bye, Didi.' I will never forget those faces peering up at me.

Despite all that had happened, I didn't want to leave. Everest to me was still a magical place, the place where I had felt most content and alive. I wanted to stay with my team too – only those people knew what we had been through. Suddenly I felt as though I was having to face the world alone.

The helicopter revved to life and the boys stepped back. We took off, spun through the air and set off down the

Khumbu Valley. Suddenly, Everest was gone, though I could still feel its presence.

The world turned green again as we flew through the valleys, mountain forests blossoming all around us. I breathed in the oxygen-rich air at 3,500 metres. The world rushed past my window. It was over.

I was going home.

CHAPTER 17

As forests and raging rivers rushed past beneath me, so many memories and feelings were flooding through my mind.

I was filled with dread at going home, desperately ashamed for putting my team at risk, and so confused at how events had spiralled out of control so quickly. And yet, I couldn't help but find myself feeling guiltily proud that we'd reached the summit. I couldn't help but smile when I thought about everything we'd been through.

Everest had brought me to my knees with tears of joy. When I saw the curvature of the Earth at sunrise on summit day, I thought I would burst. I had never felt so much happiness. And yet now, I wondered how I could cope with the crushing pain I was feeling. I thought about how selfish mountaineering was, and in turn how it had made me selfish too. How could it be acceptable to put my family through so much, and risk the lives of my team? It suddenly seemed so reckless. It was as though the bad had cancelled out any good.

I tried to reason with myself that my teammates had taken on the same risks that I had. They too had left loved ones behind in pursuit of their goal, knowing that – no matter how well prepared they were – they might never come back. We've all been reckless at some point; we've all done something knowing the consequences, but gone ahead and done it anyway.

I had stood at the foot of Everest, fully aware of the risks I was about to take, but it hadn't lessened the shock when things did go wrong. I would have to be a robot not to feel the consequences of that decision so deeply. We are only human, after all.

Ultimately, everyone will come to their own conclusions about what risks are worth taking in life. Some will argue that nothing is worth dying for, and others would argue the exact opposite. In a world where you can be struck down by a car while walking across the street, why shouldn't we take every day as a chance to seek the most visceral experiences we can? Sure, you can live to 100 years old by not leaving the couch, or ever stepping outside of your comfort zone, but as the saying goes: 'Life's not about the amount of breaths you take, it's about the moments that take your breath away.'

As mountains and raging rivers gave way to rice terraces cut steeply into luscious green hillsides, I sensed that, while right now I felt like shit, and there had been two years of highs and lows, the story of Everest wasn't over yet.

We go through life having good and bad moments, successes and failures, and we make good judgements and bad. Alongside mistakes, we can also have great moments of genius, and perhaps they can even happen both at the same time. Perhaps seeing ourselves at our worst can inspire us to be our best. Perhaps bad couldn't cancel out good, and good couldn't cancel out bad, but rather they lead on from one another – all part of this same journey that we do our best to fumble through.

Perhaps there would never be an end-point to Everest. We don't just put sections of our lives into neat little boxes and then move on without being changed somehow. Everest would affect me for the rest of my life. I knew that. So, it couldn't just end here, feeling like this. Success *or* failure, I started to consider, perhaps weren't an end-point.

I had made a huge mistake, but I still owed so much to Everest and to myself for choosing to face up to her. I thought back to my first ever climb at the climbing wall – the thrill of trying something for the first time. I thought too about my first outdoor lead climb, and that feeling of gratitude as the Dorset breeze blew in my hair. I thought about how much I'd grown with every step on Mount Manaslu; about how I'd faced my hardest days, and had come out the other side. And now, just as those highs had taught me so much, I was going to have to face up to and deal with this serious low, and learn something from that, too.

I didn't know when the mistake was made – whether it was when I agreed to go on the expedition in the first place, or when I grabbed that fateful rope, or perhaps it was when my mental and physical strength left me as we tried to descend. Whenever the mistake happened, I needed to put it right. In that moment, though, I didn't know how.

All I knew was that I was heading home to face the music, and that I couldn't expect to feel the lightness of life any time soon. Everything was just too raw. The pain for everyone was too close to the surface.

Despite the shame and guilt, though, I knew that my wounds would heal and I would eventually find my strength again. At least I hoped I would. I had come too far and seen too much to not now be a wiser and more humbled person. I hoped, too, that however Rick and Lhakpa felt about rescuing me now, one day they would feel proud of themselves for saving my life. I thought about my parents, and what I'd put them through, and I hoped too that they had seen the depths of their resilience as they'd waited those long hours by the phone to hear if I was alive or dead.

I had to hope that whatever I or those around me felt right now, it would not last for ever. I had to hope.

As we touched down in Kathmandu, I was still broken by how things had turned out, but the time to reflect had given me a little resolve. Yes, the next few weeks were going to be tough, but when this was all over, I was going to put my mistake right. I was glad I had climbed Everest, but I had unfinished business.

CHAPTER 18

I left base camp on 20 May and hours later, after I was checked out of the medical clinic, I was hauling my duffel bags up the hallway of the Yak & Yeti hotel in the heart of Thamel, the tourist area of Kathmandu. I turned the key in the door and stepped into my room.

The silence hit me. Nothing was moving in the breeze of the wind. Utter stillness. The bed was crisply made up. Light poured in from the windows. Feeling the carpet beneath my bare feet, I walked over to the bed and sat there for a few seconds, not even able to begin processing the emotions and thoughts that were still going through my mind. It was like nothing had happened – and yet, everything had happened.

I felt as if I had woken up from an Everest dream, and the emptiness of this room only served to echo my sense of feeling at a loss. I felt like an intruder in my own personal space. The silence was deafening.

I got up off the bed and walked into the bathroom. It was gleaming, freshly cleaned. Everything was so big and spacious. I caught the reflection of myself in the mirror. I hadn't seen a mirror since I'd left Kathmandu.

My face was red from sunburn, with layers of dark dead skin where I'd been windburnt. My eyes and cheeks were hollowed. My hair was a matted mess with dark roots turning to bleach-blonde rats' tails. I looked feral.

I pulled off my clothes and stood staring at my naked body in the mirror. Everything from my neck down was ghostly white – except my hands, which were sunburnt and weathered by the mountain. My ribcage looked enlarged in comparison to my tiny waist, which had been constricted by my backpack waist strap for so long. My waist gave way to skeletal hip bones but, looking at my legs, I saw muscles rippling under taut skin. Largely though, I was skin and bones. The mountain had eaten me alive.

I stared at the body that had somehow become my own. I knew what it had been through – the crushing suffocation of the death zone; the killer cold that ate its way into my bones; and then my fall, which had left my shoulder and back badly bruised. I felt as though I owed it an apology – it had served me so well, and the whole time I had no idea how much it was suffering, buried under layers of clothing for so long. I couldn't believe I'd done this to myself.

I stepped into the shower, and felt the cool drops run over my eyelids and melt into my mouth. I was alive. I kept reminding myself of that. I told myself to feel that water running over my skin.

I watched as the floor began to fill with bits of dirt, and the water tinged with brown. The mountain washing away.

I lay awake that night, running over the entire summit push in my head, questioning how it had gone from being one of the best moments of my life to the worst. The lights and noise of the city outside my window felt so alien in comparison to the cracks of the Khumbu Glacier and the distant roar of avalanches. It was almost as if Everest had never happened.

The next evening, I was lying on the concrete floor of Kathmandu International Airport in the foetal position, using one of the flags I'd taken to the summit as a blanket. My flight had been delayed and there were no empty places to sit. A thunderstorm raged outside, and hundreds of people surrounded me, fanning themselves in the humid air. I thought: *My last moments in Nepal after surviving Mount Everest, and here I am, hiding in the corner.*

I dreaded going home. I knew these last few moments in this wonderful country were sacred. I knew that I faced a media storm when I stepped off the plane – that thought was causing me more feelings of terror than anything on Everest had. I shut my eyes and tried to transport myself back to the mountain, before my fall, when I was happy and the world was good. A voice came over the Tannoy – my flight had been called. Time to leave.

On the flight I started chatting to another English person. He had been trekking in Nepal. He asked me what I'd been doing – 'Everest Base Camp?' I nodded – it was kind of true. I wondered why I hadn't told him the truth. I guess I was relishing the anonymity that I knew I would lose as soon as we landed.

At our connection in Doha, I went to one of the computers in the departure lounge and checked to see if there were any more news articles about me in the papers. There had been a constant stream every day since I'd reached the summit. It felt strange at first, seeing my name mentioned in the news, but now, having seen it so many times, I had become immune.

A new article appeared when I googled my name. *The Guardian*, the paper that I read the most, had just published an interview with Kenton, talking about my fall. I felt the blood drain from my face. *Why hadn't he asked me, or told me he'd done it?* I read the words and my heart sank – it described in graphic detail how I had been rescued 'close to death' from the mountain. I knew my parents would see this and be devastated. I had wanted to sit down with them in person and explain what had happened, but I realised in horror that it was too late.

I got on the plane to Heathrow filled with dread. I just wanted to disappear.

When the plane touched down the next morning, my head felt as if it was going to explode. My red blood cells, having multiplied in their thousands to compensate for the lack of oxygen in the death zone, were now causing my blood to thicken. My head was foggy and, as much as I was desperate to step through those doors and back into the arms of my family, I also dreaded what else was to come with the press.

The guy I had spoken to on the plane stood with me at the baggage carousel. He eyed me with confusion when I grabbed my three huge duffel bags, which looked so damaged they might have survived a nuclear blast. His luggage, for apparently the same trek, was less than half the amount. We then walked together towards the Arrivals doors and said 'Have a nice life' to each other just as a row of cameras appeared. The guy looked at the cameras and then at me. His face said it all: *What the hell?*

Sorry! I smiled back.

We walked in different directions. It was my last moment of peace before going into the media storm.

CHAPTER 19

As I turned and walked away from my fellow trekker, I was scooped into my mum's arms. She was crying on my shoulder and hugging me so tightly, as if feeling she might never have been able to hold me again. I cried at her crying; seeing her made me realise the full extent of what I'd put her through. To this day I am amazed at my parents' strength – they didn't ask to be put through any of this, and yet they have dealt with it so stoically.

My stepdad was there, too, also fighting back the tears. Somebody asked him if he was proud of me. He told me all he felt was relief. The overwhelming relief that comes when a child you thought you might never see again is back in your arms.

'Where's Dad?' I asked. I couldn't see him or my brothers. Mum told me that my sponsor had organised everything, and she didn't know that Dad wasn't going to be there. He hadn't been told about my return.

After being the one person who supported me in the beginning, my father was not there to see me when I arrived back home. I was crushed. This wasn't how it was supposed to be. None of this was how it was supposed to be. I should have made sure he was there.

Despite the joy of seeing my mum and stepdad, the upset from not having my dad there was at the back of my mind all day. I spoke to him on the phone and he sounded so upset at not being invited to the airport. I promised I would see him as soon as I could, and then we were interrupted – I needed to give an interview for Sky News.

I stood looking down the camera, wearing an earpiece so I could respond to Eamonn Holmes's questions and thought, *What the hell am I doing?*

Thankfully, I got to see my dad a few days later. He threw a party for me and invited our whole family to be together for the first time in years. Everyone there was completely shocked by the level of press attention I had received.

On the first night after I arrived home, I was sitting with my family watching the news when the headlines were read out. 'Bonita Norris, the youngest British female to climb Mount Everest has returned home today ...'. We all looked at each other in shock and my stepdad threw his hands up as if to say, 'now you're on the bloody news!' My sponsor, though, was delighted – they garnered the equivalent of £1.3 million in free advertising for themselves and their clients. I was proud of what we'd achieved as a team. The marketing and PR team had had sleepless nights planning my return down to the last detail, and I was so glad that their faith in me had paid off. They had taken a huge risk, and given me a chance. I just hoped I was doing everything I could to help them to re-coup their investment in me.

Still, for every positive article there came the bad. The comments sections underneath online articles were the worst to deal with. Keyboard warriors spoke about the destruction of Everest, saying that my ascent symbolised everything that was wrong with the mountain. They couldn't have described me any more differently than the person I thought I was. I was being painted as a scapegoat for Everest's ills, my character assassinated repeatedly in forum after forum online. I wanted to have a thick skin and be able to ignore them, but I took every one to heart.

The week after I got back, I was doing a photo-shoot for a newspaper with my mum, as they wanted a picture to accompany an article about us both.

The photographer could see how melancholy I was. He stopped and said, 'Hey, what's better – being here having all these people fuss over you, or being back in the death zone on Everest?' Everyone laughed. The answer was obvious, right? Who wouldn't choose to be in a photo-shoot for a national newspaper, with a professional make-up artist, lighting, and a journalist on hand asking questions? It was the epitome of glamour that so many sought. As people chuckled at the ludicrous idea that the death zone was favourable to a photo-shoot, I felt a deep anger brewing in my chest. I would have given *anything* to be back on that mountain with my team. If I could have clicked my fingers and been back there, I would.

CHAPTER 20

After the last article about me had been made into fish and chip paper, I found myself in my bedroom on a July day, looking at the pieces of rock I'd taken from near Everest's summit. They were just a few small stones, but to me they were moon dust – utterly priceless. I found myself asking: *Was it all worth it?*

After months of talking to everyone I knew about the expedition, I still couldn't work out how I felt about it. I had no perspective, and swung wildly from feeling euphoric at what we'd achieved to heart-wrenchingly upset about my fall. I didn't know what to think. At Base Camp after the summit, people had been reassuring me and telling me not to worry about the descent; that no one got seriously injured, and that worse things had happened. But I couldn't help but think, *It is a big deal.* My friends and family had gone through so much, but even that hadn't seemed to dampen their pride and jubilation in me achieving my goal.

Everyone assumed that now Everest was done and I had been lucky to escape with my life, I wouldn't go back to the Himalayas again. *Why would she?* Everyone had moved on, except me.

I didn't know if I'd ever go back to the Himalayas either. I'd completely lost my confidence as a climber and in my own judgement. I felt as if I was less than beginner –

because now I had so much baggage weighing me down. The intuition I'd had at the start had been replaced by shattered confidence; I didn't trust myself or my judgement at all.

I wrote in my diary: *'I have so much regret from how it all turned out. That regret will probably never leave me. What's done is done and I can't take it back.'*

My Himalayan climbing career did appear to be over, after a grand total of two expeditions. Before Everest, I'd assumed that I'd be going on expeditions to Nepal, Pakistan, Tibet and India for the rest of my life. Now, I felt almost too scared to think of those gigantic peaks. I was so undeserving of them. I tore myself apart with the thought that, if I returned, the same thing would happen. That if I tried to salvage my love of the big mountains, I would be spat right out again, but this time probably dead.

'Maybe I have had a lucky escape, and I should never try to push that luck again?' I scribbled down. I looked back up to the top of the page: *Was it worth it?*

I didn't manage to answer that question that day in my bedroom. I knew that one day I would have to deal with what was going on inside my head, and the only way I could think how was to get outside. I knew running and climbing always helped me work things out.

I spent the summer of 2010 climbing in the UK, on easy routes to rebuild my confidence. Every weekend was a new adventure; I went to Dorset, Wales, Devon – anywhere and everywhere. I'd go camping and 'trad' (traditional) climbing, and I found that when I had my nose up against a cliff face with waves crashing beneath me, it stopped me thinking too much.

Sometimes I'd go running alone in Swinley Forest. I'd reach the top of a hill and look out at the woodland beneath me, the twilight silence interrupted only by my breath and the occasional burst of birdsong. I'd realise I had tears in my eyes. They weren't tears of despair or joy, they were simply tears of gratitude – I felt lucky that I was alive and able to fight another day. I felt as though I'd been given a second chance, and I needed to make the most of it. To live life without fear. *Somehow.*

One night, I was sleeping under the stars in a cave on a cliff edge on the wild Dorset coast. The waves were lapping against the shore and the moon shone down on me and my group of friends. I thought back to when I'd slept under the stars before Everest and Manaslu, and had been so full of excitement for what was to come – for the things I hadn't seen or experienced yet. Now, I had seen all of those things, and they were just as wonderful as I'd imagined. *I want to go back*, I remember thinking as I fell asleep. Despite everyone else's logic that I'd achieved what I'd wanted and didn't need to risk my life again, I found myself thinking that, for me, Everest wasn't over yet. I was still on that journey. It hadn't ended when I stepped off that mountain.

Over that summer, I also started to fall back in love with climbing – and with climbing just for the sake of it. The things I used to know, before my fall on Everest, were starting to come back to me – like when I found myself moving over rock and ice in the Alps, that fleeting moment of being at one with the dance, feeling smooth granite on my fingertips, or the mountain breeze in my hair. Everest had been my goal, but climbing was where true joy came from. I remembered how much I loved that sense of flow and being at 'one' with nature.

I dealt with a lot of my demons from Everest summit day, and I came to terms with the fact that, regrettably, a huge mistake had happened, but the long-term effects were almost zero and, in some ways, I had learnt so much more than if everything had gone to plan.

I was getting asked to give presentations about my climb; it forced me to think about just how much Everest had taught me, and see the positives. When I spoke to others about those lessons, it gave me a chance to see those lessons as something more and more worthwhile. I felt lucky to have been able to learn them, however tough the process was. Here are those lessons learned:

Everest taught me that it doesn't matter where or when you start, starting is the most important thing of all. We have the power to trigger great change, but it takes action – that first small step.

Everest taught me about the importance of having a vision. A vision that felt so *real* that, in my lowest moments, when I questioned why I was doing something so painful or frustrating or embarrassing, it reminded me of the bigger picture, of why I started in the first place.

Everest taught me that people from Wokingham can do 'big' things. It doesn't matter where you come from, with enough self-belief, self-awareness and perseverance, you can achieve things you might not have thought you were capable of.

Everest taught me that big goals are achieved by small

and often mundane steps, but the small steps really do add up – so I should always trust in them.

Everest taught me that the world is full of opportunity if we're willing to take risks and get ourselves 'out there', whether that's picking up the phone, or by trying something new – the world is full of opportunities that we alone must realise.

Everest taught me that I shouldn't be afraid of being a beginner, because everyone started out as a beginner. Becoming an expert is a journey, and then some, and the best mountaineers I know are always learning. I am not the climber today that I was when I stood on the summit of Everest – we must always stay on the journey of learning and honing our skills.

Everest taught me that sometimes you do have to take leaps of faith, even when you don't feel ready. Sometimes you win and sometimes you lose, but every time you take a leap of faith, you learn something. Often you'll learn that you're far more capable than you think you are.

Everest taught me that when I most want to give up, I have so much more to give, even if it's just one more step. We all go through moments of wanting to give in, but those moments are transient and, in time, we will look back on that moment and be glad that we didn't give up. I learnt to push on through my worst moments, knowing that soon I would be glad I did.

Everest taught me that our imaginations have an incredible ability to freak us out and tell us we can't do things. It taught me to be wary of the voices in my mind; how I would easily find myself entertaining fatalistic ideas about things that hadn't even happened. Our imaginations can inspire us to do great things, but they also make us cower. That realisation taught me to take a step back and question where my thoughts are coming from – from my emotional, simplistic, animalistic brain, or my logical human brain?

Everest taught me that I will never overcome or be free of fear, but it did teach me that I could learn to block it out, that I could focus my attention so fiercely on the process, that I would – for a split second at least – not be so gripped that I couldn't move.

Everest taught me that the world is full of good people – the people who would risk their job to sponsor my expedition, or the people who risked their lives working on the mountain itself. There are people everywhere who are willing to put faith in you, give you the benefit of the doubt, and be kind when you make a mistake. You are that person, and I am that person too. The world is a much more forgiving and kind place than we think.

Everest taught me what is possible when we have good support behind us. Without my team and my parents, I would have found the journey impossible. It's amazing what people can do when they support each other.

Everest taught me that being connected to nature, to other people and to our own bodies, mind and purpose is what makes us feel truly alive. Possessions, successes and power have nothing in comparison to the joy you get from feeling connected to life around you. We are hard-wired to seek connection, and Everest reminded me of that – of what's truly important.

Everest taught me about the importance of going the last few per cent, of knowing that it takes a lot more than just mindless energy to achieve a goal. It takes that magical something – that true grit, when you make the decision to dig deeper or leap further into the unknown than you have ever done before. Often, when we think we've broken the back of something, there's still so much more work to do – the last few per cent is the courage to say, despite how weary from the battle we are, *we can do this*.

Everest taught me that I could draw strength from so many places, both good and bad: from fear and gratitude, connection and disconnection. It wasn't until I needed to keep finding strength that I realised just how many places it was in.

Everest taught me that I can make huge, stupid mistakes, so I should always do my best to learn from them and try and bring something good out of the bad.

Of course, I didn't need to climb Everest to learn those lessons. None of them is particularly profound. Most of us have learnt them just going through life. But I will say, I did learn a lot about myself climbing that mountain – good and bad – and that while we can face up to all kinds of mirrors, mine was Everest. I couldn't put a finger on why, and today, as a climber, I still can't work out why I knew I would love climbing before I'd ever tried it, but I do. Each person's spirit soars with a different opportunity or path in life – Everest was mine, and it was the place where I got to learn those lessons. For the next person, it will be something completely different.

I'm not sure where the change of mind-set finally cemented itself, but gradually, as the summer of 2010 fell to blistery cold winter days in Scotland and Wales, back in the snow, with hot flasks and big rucksacks, and then into another summer, I started to think about going back to the Himalayas. I was scared to put myself out there, but I'd built up my confidence enough to believe in my abilities once more. I had worked hard on my climbing skills and I had started to get the desire to test my limits again. I wasn't ready for another 8,000-metre peak. I needed to take a step back and try something smaller first, to see where I was at.

I had also been thinking a lot about Lhakpa. He was the one who was there when I fell, and I wanted to show him in person that his heroic efforts to help me had not been disregarded or in vain. Selfishly, I wanted him to see how far I'd come, so that he wouldn't always think of me as the girl who nearly cost him his life. I wanted to say sorry, because I'd never managed to after words had failed me at Base Camp after the descent, and I wanted us to go and have the climb that we'd planned on Everest – without any mistakes. I decided that I wanted to go back to the Himalayas, if only to climb with Lhakpa once more.

CHAPTER 21

Ama Dablam, described as 'the world's most beautiful mountain', sits delicately above the Khumbu Valley, where it can be gazed upon adoringly by us humans and probably the yaks and donkeys and chickens too. I had walked past it on my way to Everest Base Camp and said to my team-mates, only half-seriously, that one day, after Everest, we should go and climb it. It dominated the skyline with its perfect shark's-tooth outline, which descended into two ridge lines, making it look as if it was welcoming us with open arms. In fact, Ama Dablam means 'Mother's Necklace': *ama*, or 'mother', referred to the embrace the mountain appeared to be offering, and *dablam*, or 'neck-lace', referred to the huge hanging glacier that sat below the summit.

In some ways, the climbing on Ama Dablam is more technical than any pitch on Everest. However, its height – only topping out at 6,812 metres – meant that it was a much easier climb, simply due to the fact that climbers wouldn't need bottled oxygen, and wouldn't be wearing the cumbersome down suits, boots, mittens and goggles that the death zone demanded. The route on Ama Dablam would allow a climber to move light and fast, if they were strong enough. The challenge of this mountain, therefore, was that it demanded you move quickly and skilfully over unrelenting steep and rocky ground. It was not the big slog of Everest; it was a technical dance.

Emma, who had climbed Manaslu with me, was heading out to climb Ama Dablam that autumn with Henry Todd and two of her friends, Roz and Tim. I started texting Emma about the trip and, all at once, I found myself getting excited about the prospect of climbing with her again. I hoped that my training over the last eighteen months had paid off, because I had a bubbling excitement in my stomach. I wanted to go and attempt Ama Dablam, and I knew that Lhakpa would be there too.

The only problem was that Henry Todd was organising it. After my fall, I had been too ashamed to go and talk to him, but I also had a feeling that my silence towards him had upset him greatly. I fretted that, like everyone else, he would have judged me on my Everest performance and wouldn't want to climb with me again, or have me on his team. I didn't know if it was just all in my head, but I knew Henry – you had to earn his respect. I felt as though I was now ready to do that. I just needed the chance to prove it.

My heart was in my mouth as I made a phone call to him in September 2011 asking if I could join the trip. I didn't know whether I would get told in no uncertain terms to 'get lost', but if that was the answer, I knew the reason why. 'Of course you can come,' he said. He didn't seem annoyed with me at all; in fact, he sounded glad to hear from me. Again, I had let my imagination convince me that everybody hated me after my fall. Now, I wanted to jump in the air with delight. *This is my chance*, I thought. It was my first step towards dealing with that day in May

2010, over a year ago. I felt ready to take on this next challenge.

I managed to convince my parents that Ama Dablam wasn't a dangerous mountain (as if there was ever such a thing) and, to my surprise, they believed me! I told them that no news is good news; over the rest of my climbing career, that was always what I repeated to them. My mum assumed that, having climbed Everest, I was now invincible. Ignorance is bliss, and I'm so glad that my parents didn't realise quite what I was doing, otherwise it would have been far too painful for them to see me pack my bags again.

We left at the end of October 2011. On our first night in Kathmandu, I sat on a roof terrace with Emma and the rest of the team. The traffic was buzzing below us, and I felt as though time had flown by and I was back where I belonged.

We made it to the Khumbu Valley a few days later, and the tranquillity of life in the Himalayan foothills absorbed me once more. I didn't think of home, or the past or future; I was consumed by the present. On a frosty November morning, we got our first sight of Ama Dablam. It was stunning. The sight of it took my breath away. Knowing I was going to try and climb it made me look at it in a different light.

I wrote in my diary:

The route takes a never-ending rocky ridge line up the summit fields, where the angle is steep to the point of needing to front point on our crampons [using just the tips of our boots to balance on the ice]. The hanging glacier (Dablam) sits precariously to the left, and the final push is a near-vertical climb up steep ice and snow. The summit is crevassed and will one day collapse. The entire route is fixed with anchors which in the UK I wouldn't dream of using as protection – the Mushroom Ridge, for instance, has anchors wobbling like jelly in loose, sugary snow.

The Dablam looked terrifying: as if it was going to fall at any moment. We had heard from another group of climbers that there was a crack across the top. A crack suggested that a large section of it was ready to break off and crash down the mountain. Tragically, in 2016, a small earthquake struck near the Khumbu, and a part of the Dablam did indeed collapse. It killed Thundu Sherpa, who had been there on the night I was rescued from Everest. The mountains had yet again been proved so all-powerful: able to, on the one hand, allow life to survive, and on another, to take it mercilessly away.

To reach the top, we planned to climb straight up its icy face, skirting around the deadly hanging glacier. The face looked almost vertical.

'It looks impossible,' I said to Henry.

'It always looks steeper when you're further away,' he said. 'But when your nose is up against it, it's not so bad. I bet when we get up close, you'll see you can do it.'

I thought about the other challenges I'd faced, and he was right. Things always look worse from far away; nothing's ever as bad as you anticipate. I was scared but I was also excited at the adventure that lay ahead. Anything could happen in the coming weeks.

The first night at Base Camp, the mountain loomed over us, its white flanks illuminated in the moonlight, the stars shining around it. I couldn't believe I would ever make it to the top. Lying in my sleeping bag, I could feel its presence behind me. I couldn't help but think that this could be the expedition on which my luck ran out. But I told myself I had to keep faith. I'd spent a year and a half perfecting my skills, and I was pretty sure I was confident in my abilities once more. *Trust yourself, you can do this,* I whispered aloud.

The next day, I was emptying out a bowl of dirty water after a wash, when I saw a familiar face. Lhakpa. It was the first time we'd seen each other since Everest. He froze and I ran over and hugged him, and burst into tears on his shoulder. I could feel Everest haunting me in that moment – I still felt so much raw pain for what I'd put Lhakpa through. More than anything, I just wanted to climb this mountain to prove to him that I had learnt my lesson, and that I could get down without getting injured.

The night before we left for our climb of the mountain, Henry took me aside. He looked me in the eye and said, 'Now, Bonita, you're good at getting to the top of mountains, but you're not very good at getting down. You need to get the descent right, OK?'

I nodded furiously. I'd been thinking the same thing for so long. 'Henry, I promise you, I know it. It's all I can think about.' With that promise made, I knew there was a great expectation on my shoulders – no mistakes. Henry and Lhakpa had given me a second chance, and they wanted to see that I was worthy of it.

I shared a tent with Emma the whole way up the climb, and those evenings in the tent were some of the most hilarious nights I've ever had. We rolled about in fits of laughter talking about relationships, men, and I can't remember what else. I would almost forget that we were camped on an incredibly dangerous mountain. It was the perfect distraction from what lay ahead.

My fear of something going wrong was expressing itself in so many ways. I was the most vigilant and safety-obsessed person on the mountain. I was also militant with organisation and timings. If we said we were leaving at 8 a.m., I would be walking out of the camp at one second to the hour. I had become more diligent, more focused and alert. So far, it seemed, my accident and my ensuing training back in Europe had changed me for the better. I couldn't allow a repeat of what happened on Everest. I was aware of it with every step.

Lhakpa was always ready to go, too, and so we would trudge out of camp first and get to the ropes before anyone else – this meant nobody was climbing above us, and allowed us to move even quicker. We climbed in unison, Lhakpa and I, and the mountain. Ama Dablam had the most perfect granite I'd ever seen. Gritty and raw, giving us perfect friction. The climbing was spectacular – it was beautifully technical, and I felt as though we were dancing our way up, moving delicately, using every muscle to balance, stretch out, heave and push. The drops were exhilarating – often disappearing into an ocean of cloud below us. By the time we made it to summit night, I was drunk on my love of climbing. I felt as though my heart was nearly healed again.

On summit night, we were in the tent, making preparations, nerves steadily building, when we saw head torches coming down the mountain in the dark. Something was wrong. There shouldn't have been anyone out there at this time. Then, the radio crackled to life: a rescue mission was under way. A climber was unconscious and his teammates were trying to help him down. My blood froze. It was like Everest all over again. Though now I was watching from the tent, horrified at what was unfolding over the radio. I prayed and prayed that the man would be OK. Surely he would be? I had been.

Soon after, we saw the head torches descending quickly, and news came over the radio: 'There was nothing more we could do. He's dead.' His teammates were devastated. They were also exhausted, and needed to get back down to the nearest tent, or risk having an accident themselves. They had no choice but to leave his lifeless body up there, alone, in the dark.

That night, I lay in my sleeping bag and questioned what the hell I was doing. *Why are you here? This isn't a game. This is real. You could have been that guy; you were lucky to survive. Why are you risking it all again?*

Suddenly, climbing Ama Dablam seemed utterly pointless. Eventually, though, sleep engulfed me, and I woke up the next morning saying to myself: *Just take one step out of the tent, and then you can decide if you want to go home.*

Of course, as soon as I stepped out of the tent the next morning on our summit push, I found myself taking another step, and then another. Lhakpa was at my shoulder. We were going to do this together. Whatever it meant, whatever it gave us, we were following that desire. Still, to this day, I find it hard to put a finger on why I climb and why I take such risks in the face of death. I still don't know truly why, though all the reasons could fill a book of their own. All I knew, that day, was that it was a beautiful morning, and I was taking those small steps up that peak, and I was going to show Lhakpa what I was capable of.

We didn't know where the dead climber was, though we knew that he would be somewhere along the fixed lines and that we would most likely have to climb over him to continue on. It felt so wrong, but I reminded myself that this was the game we played – we all accepted that, every time we stepped on to a mountain, we might be left on its slopes, never to return home again.

We tried not to think too much about him – emotions are a dangerous thing in the mountains; they drain your energy and cloud your judgement. We needed to focus on our goal. After all, this was my moment of truth; this was where it could all go wrong again. I couldn't let that happen. I kept saying to myself, *You need to own this. No mistakes. No excuses. Own it.*

Those first few minutes away from the tent always feel awful. It was bitterly cold, the altitude was starting to bite; the lactic acid was building up and blinding me with exhaustion after just a few moments of effort. This struggle became my 'normal' again. It seemed as if my muscles remembered it from Everest and Manaslu, and I felt myself leaning into the pain threshold once more.

I could see the sun's rays hitting the mountain only 30 metres away. The ice blazed in luminous gold, threatening to blind us. *Just get to light*, I thought, knowing how warm it would be there in comparison to the frigid shadows. I climbed as fast as I could until, finally, I was bathed in that beautiful warm sunlight. From that moment, I knew I could do it.

Lhakpa and I got into a really good rhythm. We'd left camp first so there was nobody ahead of us on the route. It seemed as though we had the whole of this Himalayan mountain to ourselves. It was all ours. I knew that Henry would be watching us through his binoculars from Base Camp – two tiny little flecks in a never-ending expanse of white. The sun was blazing down on us, the sky was a brilliant blue, and the snow underfoot gleamed and sparkled. The Himalayas were beneath us and we were *actually climbing Ama Dablam*, I reminded myself. I felt euphoric; it was everything I had wanted climbing to be. It was paradise.

As I trudged from step to step, feeling my leg muscles working so hard and my body pushing itself to its limit, I knew I'd come a long way since Everest. I felt so strong and confident with every stride. I was focused and in control. This was what I had been born to do. I felt as though I was coming back to life.

A few hours in, our feelings of jubilation at climbing this glorious mountain were extinguished by the sight of a body ahead. He was trussed up in all his mountaineering gear, and looked as though he was just lying down for a rest.

Henry radioed from Base Camp: 'Bonita, you're about to pass the body. Stay calm, there's nothing you can do – the soul has gone.' I will never forget Henry saying those words – *the soul has gone*. To have Henry right there with us, even though he was thousands of metres below, gave me strength. I told him that we were OK. 'Just take a deep breath and keep going. You're going to be fine. I'm here if you need me.'

The climber's teammates had covered his face with his hood and he still had his gloves and boots on; so we couldn't see him at all. He was a pile of clothing, but underneath it all we knew there was a person.

I was twenty-three years old and it was the first time I'd seen a dead body that close. I'd seen mummified bodies in the mountains, but this was completely different. A human being, who – only yesterday – had been alive and thinking he had his whole life ahead of him. Now he was dead. He was wearing the same climbing boots as me.

All I could think about was his family. They might still not even know he was dead. I was a stranger and yet I was right there with him. I knew that that was wrong. It should have been his family able to reach out and touch him like I could. I had no idea who they were, but I knew they would have given anything to swap places with me in that moment. It felt so unfair.

He was tall and looked strong. I couldn't imagine how someone looking like that could be dead when I was still alive. It was the luck of the draw. It reminded me again that the moment was real; at any second, our souls might be ripped from our bodies too. *Focus*, I told myself. *Don't lose yourself. Don't get upset.*

Lhakpa patted me on the back and signalled for us to carry on. We were on the final push, and I told myself to only look upwards from now on. If I looked down at the man's lifeless body, I wouldn't be able to concentrate.

The last pitches of climbing seemed to go on for ever, up a steep wall of ice that left thousands of metres of air beneath our feet. I could see the summit – it was so close and yet so far. I would tell myself to move for ten steps, and then rest. I'd make eight and then collapse over the rope, gasping for air, feeling the sun beat down on my neck.

Soon enough, the last few grunts and kicks came, and I heaved myself over the top of the ice face, falling belly first on to the huge, flat plateau of the summit of Ama Dablam, Lhakpa one step behind me. We had done it.

We had reached the summit in only three and three-quarter hours. It was, in that sense, a perfect ascent. Lhakpa and I stomped about and took some photos of each other. Again, I have no idea why we didn't think to pose for a selfie together. I guess we were pretty tired and suffering from the effects of altitude, but still, I am so annoyed that I don't have a picture of us both there.

Then we sat down and I got some chocolate out of my rucksack. We sat in the baking sun and smiled at each other as we stuffed the gooey mess into our mouths. I gulped down some water from my Nalgene bottle – it tasted like the best drink I'd ever had. I'd come so far, I knew I had. My fall on Everest had led to this moment. Without it, maybe I would never have felt compelled to climb this peak. And I felt that Everest had spurred me on to better myself. I'd never felt so strong and confident with every step as I had done each day on this mountain.

We finished our chocolate. Behind us, a cloud cleared in the distance to reveal the black, ice-scoured might of Everest. We both stared in awe at the majesty of that mountain, even though we were miles away; it still dominated the skyline like a king surveying his kingdom.

I turned to Lhakpa and said what I had wanted to say for so long. 'Thank you, dude.' I started to choke up, but I had to finish what I wanted to say. 'Thank you for saving my life that night. I'm *so sorry* for putting you in harm's way. Thank you for everything you did.'

Lhakpa sat silently. He closed his eyes as the sun bathed his cheeks and he breathed in the mountain air. He didn't look me in the eye, he just nodded deeply. And then he looked at me and smiled. *Apology accepted.* It meant the world to me. It was almost exactly eighteen months to the day since my descent and, finally, I could feel the demons from Everest start to lift.

Henry's voice interrupted the moment, crackling to life over the radio. 'OK, Bonita, this is it now.'

'Henry, I know, I'm on it,' I said back. We got to our feet and walked back to the edge of the summit. Looking down, I could trace our route – a line of footprints in an ocean of rippling ice that glistened in the sun. It dropped for what seemed like miles, until it hit the valley floor. If anything went wrong, I knew we'd both be dead.

I looked at Lhakpa; he nodded at me again as if to say, 'Do this, Didi.' I wrapped my right arm round the rope and leant forward, my arm stretched out behind me, so that I was suspended over the edge, ready to abseil. The rope wrapped around my arm would create friction as I slid down, as long as I didn't fall and suddenly let go of it. I faced down to my nemesis – descending off mountains – and I said to myself: *You are amazing at descents, and you're going to own this.* And with that, I let my grip on the rope loosen, and I started to slowly and methodically climb down the face.

We made it all the way down to Camp Two in only a few hours. I felt my confidence soar with every step, though I wouldn't allow myself to think I was safe until it was over, until we stepped into the safety of Base Camp. My mental focus was the strongest it had ever been. I was tired and drained and fighting delirium; I had hardly eaten a thing – just some melted chocolate – all day. I swore I could feel the fat dissolving off my body. But, despite my body wanting to succumb to the tiredness, and sit down and rest, I pushed myself onwards, keeping as focused as I could. I wouldn't allow myself a second to feel emotional or, in fact, feel anything at all. I was a robot; I was a commander pushing my army to its limit. I wouldn't allow myself a moment to relax my body or mind. *Keep moving, don't stop, don't think about the pain.*

At Camp Two, I huddled into the tent with Emma, Roz and Tim, who had made the summit 45 minutes after us. Lhakpa had told me he wanted to push on to Base Camp; I was going to stay for a while, so we said our goodbyes, for a few hours at least. In the tent, Emma spread pâté on biscuits and we giggled and made silly jokes. We were all on a high after the summit. I savoured the salty taste of pâté in my mouth. There wasn't really room for us all, squashed in the tent, eating soggy biscuits smothered with pâté, but it was one of the best moments of the trip.

One of our Sherpa team, Kumar, who had been the Camp Two cook boy on Everest, was with us. I took off my new La Sportive boots, which I'd bought for the climb, and gave them to him. I decided I would wear my trainers for the rest of the climb to Base Camp – it was only across a boulder field and then a dusty ridge – the ice and snow was now behind us. I had already given my camera to Lhakpa. I wanted to give the Sherpas things I knew they could use in the mountains – or just sell on, if they preferred. Whatever they did with these items was up to them; I just wanted to show that I cared.

I reached Base Camp alone, just as the sun was setting. I had gone ahead of Emma and the rest of the crew because I felt I needed time to think about everything that had happened in the last eighteen months. I felt more than ever that my Everest journey was alive and burning brightly once more. I knew that I had just taken a huge leap forwards, and that now I was back on the right track.

All the mountains around me were glowing orange as I arrived in Base Camp, dripping in sweat and with a huge smile on my face. Pasang Tempa, our beloved cook, ran out of his tent, picked me up and twirled me round in the twilight. We both laughed aloud and the mountains laughed with us.

Henry appeared and gave me a big bear hug. 'Bonita, you've done a 360. The difference between this and Everest is a 360. Well done.'

That night, I got into my tent and, as I sank into my mattress, all the stresses and worries and doubt that I'd taken with me to that mountain melted away. Finally, I felt as if I had started to come to terms with what had happened that day on Everest, and I was making positive progress to getting back to that moment on the summit, before my accident.

I was so grateful to Lhakpa and Henry for giving me a second chance, and believing in me when I barely did in myself. It just goes to show what having good support can allow us to achieve. I thought also of the man we had passed en route to the summit, and I said a prayer for him. I'm not religious, but I do sometimes feel as though the universe is listening. I felt so thankful to be alive. Getting to climb with Lhakpa and thank him for what he had done was one of the most important moments of my life – any risks I'd taken to have that moment had been worth it.

As we flew away from Lukla airstrip back to Kathmandu a few days later, I wrote on my blog:

> This trip, this mountain, this country – taking the risk, knowing that I could fail utterly – but getting to climb with Lhakpa and thank him for what he did ... the whole experience has brought me back to life.
>
> I'm ready and psyched for the future; my love affair with the hills has been reignited and I can't wait to take on more challenges in the mountains in the years ahead.
>
> Taking the risk on Ama has brought me from the dark back into the light. Never give up on what you love. There will be good times as well as bad – and both are needed to truly live!

Our mistakes can teach us so much more than our successes can. My descent on Everest was a disaster, but it taught me one of my most important life lessons: to never accept 'failure' as final. Failure can be the best thing that can happen to us. Our biggest mistakes can push us to our greatest success.

By trying to right my wrongs, I'd had an incredible experience and made myself stronger than ever – stronger than I was even on Everest. As I wrote in my blog, I was brought back to life. My teammates had saved my life on

Everest, so should I have sat at home and never taken a risk again? Or should I show those that helped keep me alive that I would cherish every moment in life and live it to the full?

In life, disasters loom over us at every turn. You never know what's coming around the corner; whether you climb mountains or cycle to work, we are all taking risks. We are all fumbling our way through the universe, trying to make the best for ourselves and others. We will definitely all make mistakes, or others will make mistakes that will affect us. We have to accept that nobody is perfect and many situations are out of our control, and all we can do is try to keep our lives together, to learn lessons, and to move on the best we can.

As we flew back to Kathmandu, away from the Himalayas and back to the city, I looked out of the window and could see the Khumbu Valley below me, the valley that leads to Everest. This part of the world was so special to me now; I felt so connected to it. I knew I was going to be back. *This is where I'm supposed to be.* Ama Dablam had given me my confidence back, and now I was ready to take on a challenge that would rival Everest.

CHAPTER 22

As soon as I got home from Nepal and got my bags through the door, my mum told me I had a very interesting-looking letter. It was an invitation from Buckingham Palace for a reception to be held by the Queen in honour of British adventure. I managed to borrow a dress from a friend and wore my mum's jacket, and just a few days after I got back from Ama Dablam, sunburn still on my face, blisters on my feet, I was walking past the tourists, through the gates and across the courtyard of Buckingham Palace alongside my friend Geordie. *This is insane*, we giggled to ourselves.

It felt so strange being in that grand room, surrounded by gilded artworks and drinking champagne alongside a motley crew of other climbers, adventurers and sports people. *How can the Himalayas have brought me here?* I gazed around in amazement. When I was dreaming in my bedroom at university about the places climbing would take me, I never once thought it would lead to a night like this.

The grandeur of the chamber echoed the grandeur of the mountains, and if I closed my eyes, I was back in the shadow of those peaks. I felt, as I always did, guilty that I was lucky enough to be able to do this; that the real heroes – the Sherpas – were in their villages in Nepal, and no doubt there were those who would love to come and meet the Queen and be here right now. As I looked around the room, I felt totally out of my depth. *What am I doing in a place like this?* I thought. There were so many legendary climbers and explorers – from Sir Ranulph Fiennes to Sir David Attenborough. I was humbled to be in the same room, but also couldn't help but feel like a fraud.

We were introduced to Her Majesty and Prince Philip by a footman, who announced our names and gave a short introduction. As Geordie was introduced as an Everest summiteer, followed next by me, Prince Philip looked at us both and made an odd gesture with his hands. 'Together?' he said with a raised eyebrow. We both looked mortified and said, 'No!' and he winked at us as we were ushered away. Good old Phil.

The other mountaineers at the reception were asking me what mountain I hoped to attempt next. I found myself saying 'Mount Lhotse' and then being surprised at the words coming out of my mouth.

Back when I'd met Kenton all those years ago at Paddington Station, he'd told me about his desire to climb Lhotse. It sounded so far beyond anything that I could comprehend. A steep and unrelenting wall of crumbling rock and bulletproof ice, the summit so jagged and fine that you couldn't even stand on it. And yet, there I was, telling my peers that Lhotse was next.

Lhotse is the more dangerous, forgotten sister of Everest. The two mountains are joined; and indeed the route to the summit of Everest from Nepal is gained via the Lhotse face. The two summits meet at the South Col, where Camp Four on Everest is pitched. It's almost as high – only 200 metres shorter at 8,516 metres – and the climbing is much more technical. It's steep and exposed, with couloirs that cascade with shattered pieces of rock, missiles that protect the summit from being gained, and threaten to send climbers falling to their deaths. For the climb on summit night, there are thousands of metres of air to fall into and no room for error. The summit is so brittle that it is essentially a pile of loose bits of rock, which threaten to crumble in a climber's fingertips. Then there are the gusts of wind that bellow over the summit. But the big difference is in the logistics – because of its more popular sister, it is largely ignored, meaning there are fewer fixed ropes, less Sherpa support, and nowhere near as many people on summit night – the time when things are most likely to go wrong, as I knew too well.

When I was preparing for Everest, I'd heard that Rob had attempted it and turned back because his crampon broke, and he was a much better climber than me. Back then, I never would have thought I stood a chance.

But after Ama Dablam, and nearly losing my love of climbing altogether after Everest, I knew that I needed to challenge myself, and I felt as if Lhotse was perhaps a good way to express myself. I was starting to trust my own voice again. I knew that other climbers would tell me it was a step too far, but I figured, what's the worst that can happen just by taking it one step at a time? I told myself that I could just explore where it goes. Maybe I'd end up on the summit, or maybe I wouldn't get close; it didn't matter. All I knew was that I so desperately wanted to sink my teeth into another 8,000 metres for the first time in two years.

A few days after the Buckingham Palace reception, I called Henry to ask him if he would be willing to organise a team for Lhotse in the 2012 spring season, in conjunction with his annual Everest expedition. He agreed straight away, knowing that a long-time friend of his had wanted to try Lhotse for a few years. Bob Jen was from New York, the son of Chinese immigrants who had built a construction empire from scratch. He had spent his money learning to climb and slowly, over the years, had ticked off five 8,000-metre peaks. Henry told me that Bob was a great guy and a good person to have on the team. After all the support and encouragement Henry had given me, I knew I could trust his judgement. We would climb together alongside Lhakpa Wongchu and 'Young' Lhakpa. I put the phone down, and I felt that stomach-flipping sensation you get when you commit to something you are terrified of and excited by in equal measure.

The next thing to do was to sit down with my parents and tell them my plan. I told them that Lhotse was absolutely most definitely without a doubt a very safe mountain. I told them it was much easier than Everest and that they didn't need to worry about me at all, that it was basically just a trek. Apparently, I was so convincing that my parents took my word for it; in their own words, they thought Everest was the hardest thing I could possibly have done, so now I was obviously invincible.

I could only be thankful for my parents' ignorance, because I knew how much their naivety would protect them once I was gone. Like I did whenever I went on an expedition, I wrote them each a letter that was to be given to them if I died, telling them that I loved them, and not to be sad, as I had died doing something that I loved. It tore me in half, knowing that to follow my passion I had to put my family's future in jeopardy. I hoped as I wrote each letter that they would never have to read them, but I couldn't be sure of it. I had promised them I would return when I knew it was a promise that I could not make. But lying to them was a risk I had weighed up, and on balance was willing to take. I would much rather them not worry themselves sick for two months, because the odds were, I hoped, that I *would* come home and they would be none the wiser.

I took the weight of what I'd put them through on Everest seriously, and told myself that I would take no risks at all; that if it didn't feel 'right' on Lhotse, I would turn around and go home ... but ultimately I knew that the only way to take no risks was to stay at home in the first place. Even then, I mused, I could still get run over by a bus.

As I trained through the winter for my mid-March departure date, I realised that the subject of risk was on my mind more than it had ever been. Before Everest, I had been so focused on the climb that I hadn't really believed that something would happen to me – I had wrongly told myself that dying happened to *other* people. But now, with three Himalayan expeditions, many trips to the Alps, a ski trip to the North Pole and countless other climbing excursions under my belt, I couldn't believe that assumption any more. It seemed as if the more experience I gained, the more scared of the mountains I had become.

Someone once explained a mountaineer's progression of risk: when a climber starts out, they feel invincible – they don't think about death at all. Then they begin to accept that people die in the mountains, but they think that it's something that happens to other people, not them. A couple more expeditions and a little more realism sets in and they start to think, *I could die, but it's unlikely.* Then they realise, *I will die if I keep going.* This was my exact thought process, and it gave me relief to know that other climbers had gone through the same stream of thought. I guess it's the same thought process that people go through when they join the military or go down any risky path – your sense of invincibility is slowly chipped away as the horrors and realities of what you are doing sink in.

On Manaslu and Everest, I had been ignorant, and it had been that ignorance, that blind, unwavering confidence, that had arguably got me to the top. I had been fearless in some ways – terrified when a scary moment happened, but with an overall belief that I would survive. Now, it was the other way around. I was often calm in the most terrifying situations, but overall I believed that I could die at any moment.

I'd seen hundreds of avalanches with my own eyes. I'd seen seracs collapse metres in front of me. I'd passed dead bodies, and seen climbing friends gripped with grief when another friend had been killed. When I thought about Lhotse, I couldn't help thinking, *What if this is it? What if this is where my luck runs out?*

Another part of my anxiety leading up to the trip was that I knew what I was about to go through. I knew how it felt to try and breathe at 8,000 metres. I knew the suffering – the extreme weight loss, the exhaustion, the cold. I'd never been scared before a trip. Before Ama Dablam I had questioned my confidence and abilities, but it hadn't

THE GIRL WHO CLIMBED EVEREST

crossed my mind that I might actually die. Now it was all I could think about – dying and death. It was an entirely new feeling and I often berated myself for it. *What's happened to me? Why have I become so meek?*

I tried to work through my thoughts by talking to friends and other climbers, and the response was always the same: why don't you just not go, then, if you're that worried you're going to die?

It seemed like such a simple decision to make, but to me it was the most energy-sapping and emotionally draining decision I had ever had to battle with. On the one hand, Lhotse was a chance to go back to the place I loved the most, where I felt most alive and happy. On the other, it could be a death sentence. I thought to myself: *I could literally be making the decision that will end my life.* The frustrating thing was, I didn't have a crystal ball and so I would never know the outcome of the expedition unless I actually went – it could potentially be the best thing I'd ever done, or the worst. It could be a repeat of Everest, or it could be the chance I needed to prove that I wasn't the same climber I had been that fateful night. For everyone else the question of 'Why don't you just not go?' seemed so straightforward, but for me it became an agonising choice that I would lose sleep over for months. For most of the people closest to me, it seemed utterly pointless. 'You've climbed Everest, why do you need to go and do this mountain that no one has ever heard of?' But to me, Lhotse felt way more important than Everest. It felt as though Everest was just the warm-up, the introduction, and that this was the final act – the big finale, the greatest risk I would probably ever take; and I had taken my whole climbing career to get ready for it.

Throughout late February and early March, I would go for evening walks with Sophie, one of my oldest friends. We would walk around Wokingham in the dead of night for miles and miles, talking away and not noticing the hours slipping away. I would ask her all the questions I had asked myself, *Is it important enough? Do I need to prove myself? Why do I want to do this? Am I prepared to die?* Sophie was always a voice of logic and reason, and she would tell me time and time again that I was probably being fatalistic, and that if I looked at the odds, I had a very high chance of coming home alive.

I got home after one evening walk, exhausted from talking and worrying, and woke up a few hours later in the grip of flu. I lay in bed, having hot and cold flushes, my joints and bones aching, too exhausted even to get out of bed to go to the toilet. It felt as if I had a ton of bricks pressing down on my whole body. In a moment of horror, I realised that this feeling was almost as bad as how it felt in the death zone. Suddenly, all the worst things about mountaineering – the exhaustion and aching body and foggy mind and pounding head were all back with me in my bed in Wokingham. Usually, as women say with childbirth, the pain of the death zone is soon forgotten with the rush of reaching the summit. But that night, feeling so weakened that I couldn't get out of bed, I questioned again whether Lhotse was a good idea. *When is it ever a good idea to do something so dangerous when your body is so weak and starved of oxygen?*

Then the next thoughts, which gave me warmth through the shivers of a cold flush that had settled in my bones: *Why don't you just stay here and have a nice spring in the UK, go climbing by the sea?*

I fell into a fitful sleep and ended up having a nightmare. In my dream I was walking across a glacier in the mountains; as I stepped, the ground beneath me gave way to darkness, and then I was falling, with tonnes of ice and snow falling on top of me. I was being buried alive and falling to my death at the same time. I felt my stomach rise up into my chest as I rushed towards the darkness, and then I woke up gasping for air, sweat pouring down my forehead. *I can't do it. I'm not going.*

A few days later, my flu had cleared and spring was starting to appear outside my bedroom window. I was still resolute that I would stay here and watch magnolia trees blossom and go climbing along the south coast. I would have a BBQ with my friends and we would go camping at weekends, and probably curse ourselves for believing it was warm enough to only take our summer sleeping bags. I wanted to see spring here in the UK, where I hadn't seen spring since 2009, when I had still been at university. I needed to make a stance, to make my decision final, so I went online and I cancelled the flights to Kathmandu that were leaving in ten days' time. *The mountain is not worth dying for*, I told myself as I shut my laptop. I didn't feel relieved, and I didn't feel sad. I just thought, *That's it, then. Lhotse is over. It beat you before you even stepped into the ring.*

I then texted Henry to tell him my news – that I had cancelled my flights and would obviously pay him any money I owed him. As usual, Henry didn't reply. He was probably already in Nepal, his phone the last thing on his mind as he organised hundreds of bottles of oxygen, tonnes of food and a team of thirty Sherpas and Base Camp crew.

I went about life for the next few days, coming to terms with the fact that the next few months stretched before me as a blank slate – nothing exciting, but nothing scary either.

A few days later, I finally heard from Henry. He texted me saying, 'Don't be silly. Just get on the plane.' I stared at the message. I remember I was standing in my bedroom by the window. I felt the warm spring sunshine on my arm; it was so comforting and so tempting. And yet, as I stood there, staring at a message that was transporting me back to icy slopes, freezing temperatures and windburnt cheeks, I felt the pull once more. I had tasted the easy life for the past few days, and it hadn't filled me with the relief that I'd imagined. Spring would come around again next year. But, most importantly, there it was, a message from Henry, telling me to come. His words changed everything. If Henry believed in me, then that was worth something. You had to earn Henry's respect, and perhaps I'd done that. I trusted him, and if he thought I should do it, then I would.

He was so right. All I had to do was get on the plane. If I didn't like it once I'd reached Kathmandu, then I could go home. If I got to Base Camp and wasn't keen, I could turn around. If I left the tent on summit night and wasn't feeling good, I could go back inside. But for now, all I had to think about was packing my bags and rebooking my flights. *One step at a time*, I told myself. It was the greatest lesson I'd learnt on Everest, and now I was putting it to use again: *Don't get overwhelmed, just focus on the next step.*

I texted back, 'OK, I'll get on the plane,' and then I burst into tears. With my tears falling on my bedroom floor, I knew I'd made the right decision. It was the most visceral and surprising reaction, like something inside me was bursting with relief. The funny thing was that I expected this outpouring when I cancelled my flights, but I'd felt nothing. In that moment, I knew I was doing the right thing. I was giving myself the chance to roll the dice again; to be wide-eyed and open to a huge life experience. I knew with great conviction that I wouldn't change my mind again, and I wasn't going to fret about dying any longer either, because I wasn't going to be doing anything dangerous in the next hour, so I needn't worry. I would worry about dying when I was on the mountain. *Summit day is ages away,* I told myself, *just focus on the now. Get yourself to Base Camp.* I rebooked my flights, which were an eye-watering double the price of what I'd originally paid for them. I was totally skint, but I was going to live in a tent for two months – and on the Lhotse face, there wasn't exactly very much you could spend your money on.

Looking back, that moment in my bedroom when I received Henry's text was the moment that defined my mind-set towards the whole expedition. I had wound myself up, getting so scared and letting my worst fears play over and over in my mind, until I was in such a state that I couldn't take the thought of going any longer. I knew that those fears could ruin my resolve again, especially as the risks became more real on the mountain itself, so I set myself the challenge of not allowing myself to think too far ahead – to stay present and not let my imagination wander back to home, or the past or the future. For those next two months, my whole life was about nothing more than the next step, and I wasn't going to give my imagination the chance to fantasise about where each step would eventually lead. It was an exercise in *not thinking*, but it took a lot of my mental energy to learn to do that.

My experience in the mountains had taught me that things are never as bad as they seem; as Henry said on Ama Dabalm, the mountain looks much steeper and more impossible to climb from far away. As I'd learnt time and time again, the biggest mountains are often the ones in our minds. My biggest achievement with Lhotse was the fact that I had learned to control my fears. Without that mind-set, it could so nearly have been very different.

CHAPTER 23

Everything I learned on Everest – taking small steps, putting faith in the processes – I deployed to the absolute max to get myself to Lhotse. I told myself: *Just get on the plane to Kathmandu and, if you don't like it, you can turn around and go straight back home again.* We got to Kathmandu and I felt fine – good even, so I told myself to just take the next step: get on the plane to Lukla. *If you don't want to be there, you can turn back.* But at Lukla, I found I wanted to stay. And that was how I kept going, taking each day a step at a time.

It was the end of March 2012 and I didn't have to be at Everest Base Camp till mid April; I'd gone out a few weeks early to acclimatise really well, in the hope of making altitude sickness a smaller risk. My friend John was guiding a team on Island Peak, a smaller mountain in the Khumbu Valley that sits in the shadow of Lhotse. He invited me along and I jumped at the chance.

Ten days later, on Island Peak summit night, we set out at 10 o'clock in the evening. Kumar, our cook boy from Camp Two on Everest – and to whom I'd given my boots on Ama Dablam – was with us.

It was a freezing-cold night, and I could see something was not right with him; he looked cold and exhausted. I asked him if he wanted something to drink and he refused, telling me he was fine. It was the Sherpa way: *Don't accept help; always appear strong.* Eventually, I pressed my bottle of water into his hands and refused to let go until he took it from me. He relented and gulped down some of the sugary fluid. It looked as if he had not had a drink in years. He was so thirsty he kept on drinking. I couldn't believe that he'd been refusing my help.

When he handed the bottle back, I noticed that he was wearing just a thin pair of woollen gloves. I had an emergency pair of mittens in my bag, so I dug those out and gave them to him. He hugged his hands into his armpits and mumbled, 'Thank you, Didi.'

I will never forget that moment. A few years later, in the 2015 earthquake that struck Nepal, Kumar lost his life. He was survived by his wife and two children. In that moment, though, he was alive and breathing the freezing mountain air, the vapour from his breath rising around him, and behind him the sun was coming up, painting the sky a brilliant orange. He was alive.

As the sun came up, we got a view of Ama Dablam. It looked incredible in the sunrise, one of the most beautiful sights I had ever seen.

Ama Dablam dominated the skyline as we looked in awe out towards the horizon. 'Did you really climb that?' one of the team asked, and I felt a rush of pride. 'Yes, I did.' Though I could barely believe it myself. It looked impossible from our viewpoint. Seeing Ama Dablam, and knowing that I had made it to the top allowed me to think, *I can climb Lhotse.* And my spirit soared.

Two hours later, the sun was getting high in the sky, and we were sitting on the summit of Island Peak, with Lhotse towering over us like a mythical beast. It shot another 2,000 metres vertically into the heavens. The clouds parted and for a moment I could see the summit, spindrift swirling along its knife-edge ridge. I looked up with the realisation that the next challenge, now that Island Peak was over, was to try and climb Lhotse itself. I hadn't allowed myself to think about it because I'd been focusing on the small steps, and just concentrating on getting to the top of Island Peak. Now I had to face up to it: *This was what's next.*

It didn't even look like a mountain: more like a sheer wall of rock, a fortress. Grim and forbidding. It could be Mordor. It's the kind of mountain a tough, gnarly, crazy mountaineer would climb. Not people like me from Wokingham.

'So you're going to go up there?' John said.

'Probably not,' I said. 'Probably won't make it anywhere near.'

I was saying it to myself as much as to John. I knew that if I looked up too long, I would start to imagine the endless scenarios that could play out high on that peak. I felt tiny, and Lhotse felt impossibly huge. So immediately, I told myself not to even think about it. We probably wouldn't summit, so there was no point worrying about it. No pressure. We were just going to try for the hell of it.

A few days later, I was walking up a cobbled path through Dingboche village on my way to Everest Base Camp, and I bumped into Henry for the first time on the trip. At 6 feet 3 inches, he towered over the locals he passed on the pathway. We sat on a stone wall together, looking out towards Lhotse in the distance. He pointed up at it with his trekking pole and said, 'It's very dry, Bonita, very dry. It's been a really bad winter ... too warm. There's hardly any snow up there and a lot of rock fall. It's going to be really tough. OK?'

It felt as if our chances were diminishing minute by minute. But that was OK – I never told myself I'd make the summit. I only said I'd try. 'Don't worry too much about it,' Henry said. 'Just don't get your hopes up.'

I knew Henry didn't mince his words, so I believed him. I believed him when he said that it was going to be tough, that our chances were small, and if he was telling me not to worry about the future, then I wouldn't. Whatever he said, I knew I could trust him. We ducked into a house belonging to the wife of one of the Sherpas, and she made us tea in a smoky, dusty kitchen. Henry, hunched over in the tiny space, said, 'Just prepare yourself ... It will be tough.'

When I finally arrived at Everest Base Camp in the second week of April, three weeks after leaving the UK, I felt so many emotions – but, mainly, that I was glad to be back. Everest loomed over me, still as beautiful and magical as I remembered. How could I have bad feelings towards that mountain? It had given me the best thing in my life, and that was a love of climbing. I was greatly indebted to that peak, and I felt a sense of homeliness being back in its shadow. Climbing Ama Dablam probably had a lot to do with the peace that I now felt. I knew already that I'd come a long way, and now I was back to prove myself on an even harder peak.

I'd been trekking for three weeks and I smelt awful, so I had a 'shower' – a bucket of warm water. I got into my tent, fresh and clean, feeling so, so happy to be back. I wasn't thinking about Lhotse or the weather, or anything apart from how lucky I felt to be here once more – in the place where I'd felt most alive. *I could stay here for ever,* I thought. *This is home.*

The route to the summit of Lhotse is exactly the same as the route on Everest, until Camp Three on the Lhotse face; after that, the two routes split – one heads to the South Col and the summit of Everest, and the other to Camp Four on Lhotse and then its summit beyond. So, for the moment, I was essentially back on an Everest expedition. I was climbing with Henry's Everest team, including Becky Bellworthy.

Becky had been nineteen years old when I first met her, the week after I'd got back from Everest. She had messaged me to say she wanted to follow in my footsteps and take the 'youngest British woman to climb Everest' record from me. After the help that Tori James had given me, I knew I wanted to help Becky in return.

Becky had learnt to climb and had come on trips away with our group. She had even managed to get herself to Everest in 2011, on Henry's team, after finding that elusive corporate sponsor. Unfortunately, she had suffered a stroke while at Camp Two and left Everest without gaining the summit, but lucky to be alive. She had phoned me from Base Camp in tears, trying to process what had happened. I felt for her – if that had been me, I would have been devastated. I knew how much hard work and risk she had put into her expedition, and she hadn't made a mistake, not like I had on summit night. My friends and I had encouraged Becky not to give up on Everest and to try it one last time. She managed to scrape the money together again through tirelessly finding more sponsors, and now she was back on Everest, and I was there too – trying Lhotse.

People sometimes ask why I wasn't more wary of Becky, considering that she wanted to take 'my' record from me. I never felt that way – why would I try to hold on to something that was meaningless and never mine in the first place? What would I gain from refusing to help her? I knew that I had a lot of advice to offer, and I was willing to give it freely to someone as lovely and driven as Becky. Tori had done it for me, and I felt proud to be able to do the same for Becky.

Kenton was at Base Camp too. He came up to me and said, only half-jokingly, 'You do realise Henry's never put anyone on top of Lhotse?' If anything, those words spurred me on. I wanted to climb it for Henry just as much as I did for myself. As I fell asleep that night, I could feel Lhotse looming over me – a shadow of both fear and wonder. I dreamt of falling down collapsed crevasses.

We began our acclimatisation rotations, heading up and down the Khumbu Icefall again, crossing the ladders and spending a few nights each at Camp One – where I ended up eating all my food that night with a toothbrush as I had forgotten to take a spoon or a cup – and Camp Two, where thankfully Pasang Temba cooked and I didn't have to swallow down tuna mixed with toothpaste.

The next day we planned to attempt to tag Camp Three. That night the winds were so ferocious that our tent was almost flat to my face. We could hear the roar of the jet stream up on the Lhotse summit slopes. Down at 6,400 metres, it was as if our tent was being attacked. I cowered down into my damp sleeping bag, praying that the winds would die before dawn. We had no such luck, and I had only a pair of Lycra leggings to keep me warm.

The one advantage to wearing Lycra in katabatic winds is that you move like you've got a rocket up your arse. I stomped up to the bottom of the Lhotse face so fast I could have been at sea level. Stopping to put our crampons on, though, was 'suffering' defined. I froze within seconds – my thighs had already gone numb. I shouted over the roar of the wind to my climbing partner, Paul: 'I can't feel my fingers!' He helped me with my crampons, I helped him with his helmet, both of us frustrated with our inability to move our fingers and thumbs to fiddle with fastenings and straps. It was awful. We began climbing up to the start of the ropes, but my heart was telling me that this was a bad idea – with winds this strong and the face so exposed, I would likely suffer a cold injury on my hands or feet. The winds were likely to dislodge loose ice and rock, and there were a lot of people jostling for a position on the lines. Alarm bells were ringing; I turned back without hesitation, and made a mental note to pack my synthetic trousers at all times in future.

Unlike in 2010, it felt as if there was an underlying tension in Base Camp – that people were more scared than usual. Everybody was worried about how 'dry' the mountain was; how the lack of snow would mean that climbers would have to scratch their way up blank walls of impenetrable ice, and then delicately climb over pitches of crumbling rock. There was no snow to cushion the mountain. It was totally exposed. The rumours got worse by the day – the

Sherpas were concerned about the warming temperatures and the hanging seracs over the Khumbu Icefall. We were also worried about the sheer number of people on the mountain – considerably more than in 2010; it seemed as though the route was almost bursting at the seams. It had not been like this when I'd first set foot on Everest. Everything felt different now. *Oh well,* I thought, *perhaps it's not supposed to be this year.*

One night at Base Camp, a crevasse exploded open and tonnes of ice and rock were gobbled into the darkness. The crater left behind was the size of a house, and our tents were perched alarmingly close to the rim. For the whole expedition, we had a sinkhole next to us, a reminder of just how precarious life on the mountains could be. If that hole had opened up a few metres closer, we would have all dropped to our deaths while sleeping in our tents.

One afternoon at Camp Two, I was drinking tea in the mess tent; Pasang Tempa and Kumar were standing by the tent door. Suddenly a deafening roar came out of nowhere and the ground started to shake violently. It was the loudest avalanche I'd ever heard. Pasang Tempa and I looked at each other and I knew we were thinking the same thing: *We are going to die.* In less than a second, we launched ourselves away from the sound and threw our bodies across the other side of the tent. As if that was going to make any difference. But our instincts to dive for safety were so strong. It must have all happened in just a few seconds, but I remember it in slow motion: the noise, the terror on everyone's face, and then the moment we realised that the sound had been going on too long – and we weren't about to be buried alive.

We ran out of the tent to see a huge avalanche burying Camp One. Hundreds of tonnes of ice were coming down off Nuptse and burying the entire camp. It looked as if the onslaught would never end. As their black shapes disappeared, it felt as though I was watching person after person being buried alive. We had been at Camp One that morning. It could so easily have been us.

We grabbed our equipment and ran down the Western Cwm to try and help – but thank God, no one had been badly hurt, except a man who had bitten into his tongue when he got blasted backwards in the aerosol blast caused by the amount of ice displacing air as it hit the glacier. As I walked back up to Camp Two I thought again, *I don't need to die on this mountain.*

On the journey down to Base Camp the next day, I was with Paul, one of Henry's Everest team members. We padded along through the Western Cwm in the pale morning glow, only our footprints breaking the eerie silence. I never failed to be astounded by its beauty. A pristine world cut off from civilisation by the notoriously dangerous Khumbu Icefall.

In the icefall, we were helping each other across the ladders over the gaping crevasses, and as we approached one of the first on our long descent, Paul grabbed the ropes and took the lead. Immediately, he paused as he stepped on to the ladder. I didn't ask why; I guessed he'd just 'had a moment', like we have all had crossing those beastly things. He got to the other side and turned to me, the colour drained from his face. He said slowly, 'When you cross this ladder, don't freak out. Just keep moving, keep walking towards me.'

I stepped on to the ladder and looked down. The whole wall of the crevasse was covered in bright-red blood that glistened in stark contrast to the innocent white of the ice. I had never seen anything like it in my life. I gulped for air, 'Oh my god ...!' and felt my legs turn to jelly. 'Come on,' Paul said, 'just keep walking.' I made it to the other side. Both of us were in shock and we agreed to 'get off this bloody mountain as fast as possible'. We ran all the way through the icefall back to Base Camp. I didn't stop or look over my shoulder once. The blood was from a Sherpa. He hadn't clipped into the rope and he had tripped on the ladder, smashed his head and then fell to his death. We all sat in silence at Base Camp after hearing this. Somehow, it felt as though the mountain was telling us to leave. The avalanche was a warning, and the blood across the crevasse marked the point beyond which we should not dare to go. It was as if the mountain was trying to tell us something. *Climb at your peril.*

We left Base Camp shortly after and headed down into the valleys to rest and recover, and decide on our next move – it was already the second week of May and time was running out for a summit push, but we had no choice but to wait patiently and hope that the weather and conditions would change. We walked all the way back down to Namche Bazaar, the main village and trading crossroads in the Khumbu. The air down at Namche felt like being back at sea level – we were now only at 3,400 metres compared to Base Camp's 5,300 metres. In the hustle and bustle of the markets and cafés and tea houses, Everest and Lhotse suddenly felt like a parallel universe again, but all of us could feel the mountains looming over us, much as we tried to focus on our hot chocolates and freshly baked pastries.

Hundreds of trekkers were passing through Namche too, and we looked so battered and bruised compared to them, with their flashy new trekking clothes and shiny boots and backpacks. To the trekkers, Everest was a place to be marvelled at and looked upon in wonder. But we saw its true colours – the avalanches and the death and the terror in our teammates' eyes when we thought we might be buried alive. But for a few nights at least, we could put that to the back of our minds and have a beer with a group of trekkers and see Everest in the same light they did.

It was in Namche that we heard the news: Russell Brice was pulling his Everest team off the mountain. Russell was the biggest operator, and his logistics were vital for all of us. All the teams at Base Camp relied upon and co-operated with each other. Russell was a leader whom everyone looked up to. If he was saying it was too dangerous, then it probably was. He was convinced that there was going to be another avalanche and, if there was, he had 100 people on his team – who were mostly Sherpas – and surely some of them would be caught in it. For him, the risk was too much. He pulled out, and his whole team had no choice but to pack up and leave.

As soon as I heard the news I thought: *Well, that's it.* If Russell was pulling out, then Henry would too, as they were good friends. Our expedition was over. I knew it, I had known it all along – we had never had any expectation of getting to the summit after seeing how bad the conditions were. As I contemplated what had happened, I didn't feel particularly sad. I felt as if I'd tried my best, and now the decision was out of my hands. *It's just not our year*, I thought. *Lhotse's not meant to be this time.* I made a plan to trek back to Base Camp the next day and pack my bags.

Once news got out that Russell was leaving, the rumour mill went into overdrive, and – like dominoes crashing – other Lhotse and Everest teams pulled out behind him. So many people were leaving, and sharing on their blogs the news. I started getting messages from climber friends: 'Please don't go back up the mountain. It's way too dangerous.' I got a message from a girl on Russell's expedition: 'Anyone who's staying behind is suicidal, please don't go back up there.' I knew she was right. Lhotse was not worth dying for.

I texted Henry to tell him I was coming to get my bags and go home. I was expecting him to text back and say that it was over, and yes, I should come and get my bags. But to my complete surprise, Henry texted back to tell me that he was staying put. Russell's decision hadn't swayed him. Henry had worked on Everest for over thirty years, and he was making his own judgement call, despite the pressure around him from all the teams who were abandoning Base Camp in their droves. 'Get back to Base Camp and we'll take it from there.' He wasn't saying that he thought we had a chance at the summit; he was just saying: we don't have to give up *yet*.

I was shocked, but also in awe that he would make that decision, in the face of all that pressure. I felt inspired to follow Henry's lead and to continue what I'd been doing all along. *I will take small steps, one day at a time. I'll go back to Base Camp and just see what happens.* That way of thinking lifted the pressure off again – the difference between thinking we *had* to get to the top and thinking we'll *just see what happens* is amazing. One was paralysing and overwhelming, the other offered the chance to take a deep breath and say, *One more step. No big deal.*

When I texted back to my friends and peers that I wasn't leaving, that I was going back up to Base Camp and would try and climb again, the reaction was fierce. 'Don't listen to Henry, do what's right, trust your instincts,' said one. 'You know the right decision is to turn around. Don't let Henry force you up that mountain.' The funny thing was that Henry was the one actually looking at the situation at Base Camp, and the people texting me telling me it was too dangerous were nowhere near the mountain. I didn't think we were going to make the summit, but my instincts weren't telling me to go home. They were telling me to trust Henry, and to take it one day at a time.

Back at Base Camp, we waited around for a few days. The weather started to clear. We hurriedly worked out our logistics and spoke aloud about the prospect that we might actually make it back up to Camp Two. And that was how it started. The weather held and we got to Camp Two, and from there the Everest team attempted to go for the summit, praying that the blue skies and low winds would hold. Bob and I went back to Base Camp – we couldn't go to the summit of Lhotse at the same time because there weren't enough logistics for both ascents to happen together.

On 19 May, we waited and waited at Base Camp, until finally the news came crackling over the radio – the team had done it. Becky had reached the summit of Everest, and she was now the youngest British woman to have stood on top of the world.

A few days later, I was standing outside our mess tent, watching Becky pick her way through Base Camp, looking utterly exhausted but so very relieved. She came up to me and I gave her a hug. 'I'm so proud of you,' I said through tears. I really was in awe of her – to have managed to make it back to Everest for her second attempt at the age of twenty, and after a stroke, was incredible. She deserved the record more than I ever had. She climbed the mountain brilliantly.

Becky only had the record for a day; Leanna Shuttleworth, aged nineteen, made it to the summit the day after. Leanna still has the record and she'll probably have it for a very long time. I didn't envy Leanna – she got back down to Base Camp and the press had gone crazy over her ascent. She was getting phone calls at Base Camp from journalists and, like me, she wasn't prepared for it. She was in the eye of the storm, and I could only hope that it would die down soon for her.

Now, with the Everest team done, the pressure was on Bob and me to get to the top of Lhotse. I say pressure – it was mostly friendly banter at night in the mess tent. Amazingly, the good weather that had allowed the Everest team their chance was holding, and duly, we packed our bags.

That morning, I picked up a handful of rice at the altar from our Puja ceremony and threw the grains into the crackling juniper fire that had been lit to ensure our safe passage on the mountain. This was it. We were going to try for the summit.

It was just before dawn and Base Camp was eerily quiet.

I had tried to stomach some porridge, but nerves had diminished my appetite. Instead I drank three cups of coffee and began to feel adrenaline seep through me as I visualised the climb ahead.

We clattered over tents and rocks in our high-altitude boots, weaving our way up to the mouth of the icefall. It stood defiantly, as if guarding the treasures of Everest and Lhotse beyond. I remembered when I'd stepped out of the icefall for the final time on my 2010 Everest trip and said to myself, *I never have to go up there again.* Well, now I was back – and I was about to attempt the most dangerous and difficult climb of my life. I vowed I would never go up again, if it would just let me pass safely this last time.

With little drama, Camp Three was reached, and finally Camp Four after four days. Everything had so far gone to plan. We reached Camp Four on 25 May and I had to pinch myself as I settled into our little tent and watched as the sun went down over the Western Cwm. I couldn't believe we'd got this far. Our tent was perched precariously on the steep upper section of the Lhotse face, with one side of it literally hanging off the edge. 'Don't roll over,' Lhakpa said to Bob and me. He was worried our weight would dislodge the guy ropes, and send us flying down the face for 2,000 metres.

Then Henry radioed from Base Camp: 'The weather's too bad, you're not going tonight.'

We boiled snow, ate some chocolate, and began to doze with our oxygen masks slowly pumping out on a low flow rate. We were at 7,800 metres. As I took a photo from the porch of the tent, of a crescent moon underlined by a scar on the horizon of pink dusk light, with the white peaks of huge Himalayan mountains below, cloud swirling about them, I realised that I was back on top of the world again.

Bob and I spent the night fretting about whether the weather would come good, or whether we would be spat off the mountain, having got so close. The next morning, Bob woke me up, his head peeking out from under his sleeping bag and his eyes half asleep still. 'Hey Bonita, you know what I really want right now? I want a glass of chilled white wine, and a slice of lasagne from my and my wife's favourite Italian restaurant in New York.' As he described how good this lasagne was, I felt my belly ache for home. Where we were, perched on that face, was so far removed from our normal lives, we might as well have been on a different planet. Lying in the damp sleeping bag and telling Bob how my nanny makes the best boiled eggs and soldiers for breakfast, and describing my mum's Sunday roast, I suddenly got scared. What if I never saw them again? We were about to embark on the most dangerous 24 hours of our lives. I prayed I would get to see them. I wanted to be home so badly it physically hurt. But before I could go home, I had to keep going up, and I had to stay focused.

The day of the 26th passed far too quickly – at extreme altitude, everything takes four times as long as at sea level. Boiling snow is a nightmare; most of the water it produces boils off far too quickly, which leaves a sheet of frozen condensation inside the tent and makes everything damp. It takes forever just to produce one cup of drinkable water, and then there's a high chance (sod's law) that you will knock it over before you even take a sip.

Finally, the call came from Henry. 'You're going tonight.'

We were to leave before midnight, with the aim of

reaching the summit at sunrise. There were no more nerves – we had to sort our kit out, make sure everything was dry, make sure we were fed and watered and that blisters were plastered over. A brand-new fresh pair of socks was produced; oxygen masks were securely fastened.

The moment came, as it always did, to leave the tent – at exactly 11 p.m. and not a second later. After the hours of apprehension and worry about all that could go wrong in the death zone again, I found it exhilarating to step out of the tent into the darkness and breathe the cold mountain air. Standing outside the tent in the pitch dark with Lhakpa, marvelling at a beautiful line of what appeared to be stars snaking up into the sky. Those were the head torches of the Everest climbers, making their way to the top of the world only a few hundred metres away. I was so glad to be standing with Lhakpa alone on our peak, as opposed to jostling my way to the top with all those crowds. With just the four of us climbing that night, it was perfect. I looked at the queue on Everest and I thought about how far I'd come since I was there.

As I took my first step up the face, I couldn't quite believe that we were actually here – this was Lhotse summit day, and the death zone awaited us. I was first in line; there was nothing between me and the summit. I stepped again, and soon fell into a rhythm that went on for hours. We were actually on our way. All the fear and nerves had gone – it was time to just do it.

Beyond the few feet illuminated by my head torch, I could see nothing but darkness ahead, but I always had the sense of the huge black summit ridge looming above me. As we climbed on, the route branched to the right, and the ice gave way to loose, crumbling rock. We traversed ever so carefully around a rocky band, holding on to the rock for balance, and placing every footstep down as if we were walking on glass. I couldn't see it, but I knew the drop below was over half a mile long.

The traverse ended as we entered the notorious Lhotse Couloir. The stories I'd heard of falling rock, sheet ice and pitches of vertical rock were enough to make my heart race. *No mistakes here*, I told myself. We began climbing steeply upwards, trying to find the safest passage, and work out – at anchor points – which of the many tattered ropes would be safest to clip on to.

The narrow couloir was actually oddly comforting. It was as if the mountain was protecting me from the elements and the exposure. Every time I looked up, I could only see more rock and ice stretching up into the heavens. This face was huge, and it felt as if we were making painstakingly slow progress.

We didn't stop once; after four and a half hours, the comforting enclosure of the couloir was beginning to slip away and we found ourselves back on ice. Looking up, we could see the rocky summit; looking down, we could see the Himalayas spread out like a toyland below us. As for the breathtaking exposure, every time I looked down at my feet, I could see the drop for miles below. We were on the open summit fields. I had never thought I would get this high.

Dawn was approaching and the mountain turned a pale grey. However, as the sun rose from behind the face, its precious rays were completely blocked – we were still climbing in the dark of Lhotse's shadow.

As we climbed the last 50 metres to the summit, I spotted something up ahead. I knew what it was. I had seen it so many times before. It was a person. A Czech man who had sat down only a few days before. He had not managed to get up again, and had died looking down on the most incredible vista on earth.

I found that for the first time I was able to hold back the tears, so used was I now to coming across the dead. My reaction sickened me a little. In reality this was a devastating sight. I said a prayer for his family, and then, without further ado, clipped at the next anchor and carried on.

It was only when I was about to start climbing up the very last pitch of rock that it hit me that we must be in the death zone. I didn't know the height but a good guess was that it was well above 8,000 metres. Wow. I didn't feel like I was in the death zone at all. I assumed that Lhakpa had turned my oxygen right up; when I asked him he told me that it was on a flow rate of 2.5 litres per minute, 1.5 litres less than what Henry had recommended we climb on!

I slid my jumar up the rope, let go of it, and tentatively placed my feet and hands on the rock, then I slid the jumar up again and placed my hands and feet a little bit higher. I was totally consumed by concentration. Every placement had to be perfect. The Himalayas were spread out below to my left, and below to my right was the Czech man. My mind was blocking both out – all I could see was my hands, feet and the rock in front of me.

My concentration in overdrive, I didn't even realise as I started punching my feet into the ice dome of the summit.

I clambered my way up those last few metres, and only came out of my trance when the brilliant orange rays of the morning sun hit me in the face. I screamed! And from somewhere in the back of my mind, it hit me that it was 26 May, and I had left the UK on 26 March. Sixty-one days to reach the summit. I fell to my knees and looked down the sheer drop on the other side – the east face of Lhotse dropping for miles into the valleys of Tibet below.

The tears then came. I was alone on the tiny summit, looking out at the most incredible sunrise. The entire world seemed to be at my feet – huge Himalayan peaks so small in the distance, Everest to my left, the clouds rolling below me like an ocean, and the beautiful orange and pink colours of the dawn sky illuminating the curvature of the Earth. I was the only person in the whole world who had this view. It was the most breathtaking moment of my life – literally, it took my breath away.

Lhakpa came up behind me and we hugged. It was another first summit for him too. We could see people climbing up on Everest, but where we were, there was nobody. We sat for a while and just took in the view, until Bob and the other Lhakpa reached the top. We all hugged again – four tiny humans perched on top of this giant Himalayan peak.

I realised that we hadn't radioed Henry once the entire night. I borrowed Lhakpa's radio and spoke through tears. 'Henry, we've done it – we're on the summit,' and I heard him chuckle down the radio, 'Well that's exactly where you're supposed to be.' It was typical Henry. He had been awake all night waiting on the news. 'I wish you could see what we can see right now,' I said. 'It's the most beautiful place in the world.'

'I wish I could too. I'm sure it's absolutely beautiful. You deserve it. Get down safely. Remember Ama Dablam – no mistakes.'

Henry had become such an important figure in my climbing over the years – from my first ever foray on to fixed lines on Manaslu, where he shadowed my every move, to comforting me over the radio on Ama Dablam when we passed the dead climber. Now, I wished more than anything that he could share this moment with us, and not just be a voice through the radio. He deserved to be here more than anyone. It was Henry who had held his ground when everybody else was leaving the mountain, and it was Henry who had told me to keep my nerve and just take the expedition one day at a time. I was so lucky to have a great mentor in Henry. It's amazing what can happen when someone believes in you, even when you're not sure you believe in yourself.

For the first time ever, I didn't want to leave the summit. It felt as though I had never had to overcome such a personal battle before. All the angst and worry, all the doubt and fear and homesickness, all the questioning of myself – it had been a stressful few months, and a harrowing expedition, but being up on that summit had changed everything. It's funny how just a single moment can do that – wipe out months of negativity in a single second. It had all been worth it.

I knew as I left the summit that I would never see that spot again. I had only been there a few minutes but it had given me so much; it had reminded me to believe in myself, to take risks, and to keep fighting even when success looks impossible. Throughout the entire descent I had to pinch myself and remind myself that it wasn't a dream. We had become so convinced of failure that success could not sink in.

The descent was amazing. I told myself that it was my strength. *You don't mess up on descents, you're good on descents,* I kept repeating. We made it back to Camp Two that afternoon. I had been on the go for 18 hours, with just a litre of water and no food, carrying a heavy pack in the dead zone. By the time I reached Camp Two, I could hear water, I could smell water, I wanted to eat snow, I was so dehydrated and delirious – but camp was only a few more minutes away. I arrived and dropped my heavy pack to the floor, full of relief. Kenton was there and said, 'Nice one, Norris.' It meant a lot coming from him. A year later, Kenton climbed Lhotse too, nearly four years after telling me about it at Paddington Station.

Two days later I broke down in tears again as Lhakpa and I took off our packs at the bottom of the Khumbu Icefall, in the safety of Base Camp. I had dreamt of this moment – the moment when you realise that you will never have to risk your life again on that mountain; the moment when your thoughts can finally turn to home. Lhakpa was also visibly emotional – he, too, could finally go home. I sipped my water and it tasted so good. I was alive, we were all alive, and it was over. Thank God.

Within days our Base Camp was being packed up and it was time to go. Another season over, it seemed as if we had been there for a lifetime. I looked around at the faces in our camp before we started our long journey home. For me, these big mountains are achievable because of a highly skilled team of Sherpas, and because of Henry Todd, Kame Nuru and a good team of people to climb with. No matter what the mountain threw at us, we were able to take it on. Being a part of a team like that is a great feeling. I hated saying goodbye to them – despite having taken so long, the expedition was suddenly over all too soon.

Lhotse was the hardest trip I'd ever done. The whole season was hard, with the mountain out of condition, strong weather systems, avalanches, and entire teams packing up and leaving early. But it was the mental struggle that was the hardest. I so nearly didn't make it to the mountain at all, and when I did, every day someone told me, you're never going to make it, it's never going to happen. It was the first time I'd been tested like that. On Everest, there was so much positive energy about it; everyone had said we were going to make it. This time, I was on my own. It was so isolating to be on the mountain, surrounded by people who thought I was mad even to be there.

It would have been easy to give up. But by telling myself I didn't have to think about anything but the next moment, I found the ability to carry on. I had reason after reason to go home – the avalanche, the weather, the voices telling me I couldn't do it – and, even to me, the chances of making it seemed tiny. But I never lost faith in the fact that it was possible. I just kept going, never knowing how the trip was going to turn out, and I ended up on the summit.

My biggest achievement wasn't the summit, it was to trust my own instincts and not follow the crowd.

For Lhotse, I wanted my return home to be the return I never had with Everest. Everest got taken away from me with the media storm, and after that I had promised myself *never again*. I told my dad I wanted him to collect me from the airport – no other fuss, just him.

I stepped off the plane, wandered through Arrivals, still stinking of yak butter and sweat-caked clothes, and saw my dad. I ran forwards and we hugged. Nobody standing around us knew what we'd been through in the last two months: me battling my way up the world's fourth-highest peak, and him a father waiting to hear if his daughter would come home alive.

'I'm so proud of you,' he said. And I was proud of him. I was so proud of my parents for coping so well with a nightmare daughter. We walked out of the airport into the summer sunshine. It was a glorious evening and, as we drove away from the airport, I couldn't believe how green everything was after seeing nothing but dust and ice and rock for so long.

My dad asked me what I wanted to do, and I said, 'Go to Nanny's.'

We drove to her cottage in Sunningdale, and she was given orders over the phone to put some dinner on. My nan had a beautiful little old cottage, with lovely gardens full of lavender, honeysuckle and rose bushes. We sat in her garden until late, listening to the crickets buzzing. We had pizza and a glass of red wine and everything felt wonderful. No fuss, no big grand entrance, just being with the people I loved. That was all I had wanted with Everest and I never got it. Now, Lhotse could become my Everest.

'Are you going to climb another one?' my nan asked.

The question hung in the air and I found myself thinking carefully about my response. I felt the last rays of the evening sun on my cheeks and inhaled the sweet scent of lavender and roses from the flowerbeds. I felt content. For the first time since I'd sat in that lecture and Everest had slapped me round the face, I was ready to take a step back. I didn't need to prove anything to myself any more, and I felt incredibly proud that I had got to this point, without giving up, when I thought so many times I should.

Since that lecture, I had gone from a teenager to a young woman. I had seen the roof of the world and I had learnt lessons from moments of despair that I thought might never end. I had faced death and seen the dead, but I had also felt so alive that I knew with so much certainty that climbing was what I had been put on the planet to do. That kind of contentedness only comes after years of uphill struggle. I was at the top of the highest mountain of all, and the view was so much better because of all the struggles that had come before it.

I had also made lifelong friends, and honed a skill that would unlock special places around the world for the rest of my life. I would always be able to climb a mountain or a rock face, and see Earth from a whole new perspective. I had also seen just how much I was capable of, how deep my reserves were, and how rewarding it could be to have faith in myself.

And then there were the lessons, so many lessons learned, which I felt privileged to have unlocked and could now take with me through life. Mainly, that my most crushing failure could motivate me to my biggest success.

But, most importantly, after all I'd seen and been through,

I was lucky enough to still be alive. Risking it all in the mountains had shown me that perhaps living life to the full didn't need to mean living life to the extreme. It meant drinking up every moment with your loved ones, appreciating the simple things in life – like the smell of grass when you lie in a field on a summer's day and look up at the clouds.

True living didn't mean walking the fine line between life and death. Lhotse had taught me that everything I had was right there waiting for me, as long as I had the right attitude and kept my eyes open to the beauty of being alive. I was so grateful to the mountains for welcoming me with open arms; for waking me up to how incredible and enlightening life could be when you're faced with your own mortality and really living at the limit. But, I also knew that there were other things in life which were more important to me that didn't involve stepping out of my comfort zone at all – family, friends, laughter – and now I was lucky enough to be able to embrace those things wholeheartedly. No one close to me had ever asked me to prove myself.

I sat there and thought about my nan's question, and I said, 'Not for a while, at least. There's no rush.'

We sat and drank wine, and watched the sun set, and then my dad drove me to my mum and stepdad's.

We drove past the Bracknell Athletic Club, and I looked out through the window at the old visitors' stands and terrapin block, and imagined myself as that twelve-year-old girl, running my heart out around that track. I thought back to the days I'd run along country roads with Rob in the baking sun, and him telling me that I had the choice *to be a runner or a very good runner*. I'd learnt, then, that my body was capable of great things when my mind willed it. And throughout everything I'd been through, I had come away knowing one thing for certain: our minds are the greatest tool we have. Our minds can imagine us on the tops of mountains and will us to keep going when we are desperate to give in. Our minds can be our worst enemies and our best friends.

I had lost my confidence twice – with my eating disorder and then after my fall on Everest – and I felt overwhelmed with gratitude that I'd somehow managed to find my faith again.

I wrote on my blog after Lhotse: 'You fall and you pick yourself up again – you learn your lessons and you come back stronger. That's life.'

If the mountains had taught me anything, it was that we shouldn't be afraid to fail. If you're afraid to fail, you might never take that first step. Ultimately, not taking that first step is the biggest failure of all, because that way you deny yourself the journey, and the opportunity to learn something about yourself and the world around you.

Facing up to the world's highest mountains had taught me that the individual steps are not that scary and, when they were, that I could take leaps of faith and block fear out. If you don't reach your final goal, or that goal turns into a nightmare, the journey along the way will still burn brightly and affect you in ways you could never imagine at the start, with new friendships, memories, skills, and doors opened that you never knew existed. Fear and the fair of failure never go away but, despite them, people have achieved great things.

As we drove home that night, I wished for myself the

courage to always find a way to take that first step into the unknown, to never dismiss a journey before I had started on its path. To not be afraid to fail.

And I wish that courage for you.

Take that first step. You never know where you might end up.

Dust and sweat glistened on my body, but my fingers were the worst – they were leaking sweat. *I wish I'd worn a T-shirt*, I thought, as I wiped my soaking hands on my gleaming body. I was only wearing a sports bra and shorts in the searing Thailand heat.

Below me, the rope I'd knotted to my harness swayed in the breeze, its weight threatening to pull me off my delicate stance. It fell downwards for 10 metres until it snaked into a belay device held in my boyfriend's hands.

Adrian shouted up to me, 'You can do this!' I didn't dare look down at his face. I forcefully blew air out of my lungs, as if I was trying to exhale the fear that was gripping me. Dust and chalk blew in my face. I tried not to cough. If I coughed I would be spat off and take a fall nearly to the ground.

My left hand was pinching a matchstick-head-sized pimple of rock in the cliff face. I held it between the edge of my thumb and my index finger, pushing with my thumb and pulling with my finger, trying to keep my balance as I wobbled back and forth on two tiny sloping footholds that threatened to give way at any moment. My right hand was stretched out to my right side, almost as far as it could go. And I was trying to pinch a flattened, glassy-smooth ripple in the rock. It wasn't a hold, but it was the best I had. Every time I squeezed it, to try and secure my grip and move my weight across, sweat poured from my fingers and soaked into the rock, and my hand just slid off.

My heart was thumping in my chest. I wished I could reach down and dip my hand into the chalk bag that was tied to my waist, but every time I took my hand off the wall of rock, I felt the weightlessness of my body falling backwards into space. I had to hold on, with my fingers pumping out sweat, and make the move. All I had to do was stick to that hold, pull myself towards it and shuffle my feet over. Then I'd be able to grab a 'thank god jug' as we call it in climbing vernacular – a big fat handhold that I could grip on to all day if needs be. But, right now, that jug felt so far away. I had to make one more move along this traverse, and yet I was frozen with fear.

Behind me, long-tail boats cruised through the crystal-clear waters of Railay Beach. Trees rustled in the wind and I could hear a group of monkeys calling to each other not too far away.

Adrian and I had been in Thailand for a few weeks by this point. We were tanned and fit and strong from climbing nearly every day. I didn't know it at that moment, as I clung to the cliff face, but he had a diamond ring in his pocket, and was planning to propose to me the next day.

We'd been through a lot in our year-long relationship, and this holiday was our chance to relax – if you can call being paralysed with fear and clinging to a cliff face relaxing!

We had begun dating in 2015 and, shortly afterwards, I told him that I was planning to climb K2, the world's second-highest mountain. It was also known as the world's most dangerous peak. I didn't believe that fact, and I still don't, but nonetheless it was a big step up from even my climb of Lhotse.

Our team didn't make it to the summit of K2. It was a rather harrowing experience. I got altitude sickness and then the rest of the team were thwarted by a huge avalanche that obliterated two of our camps. Just by the grace of god, nobody had been on the mountain that day. If the avalanche had come down earlier, it would have killed every single one of us.

I'd come back from K2 immediately determined to return but, after a while, I realised that perhaps my values were no longer in the same place they had been when I was twenty. Now pushing thirty years old, and with someone I loved and wanted to grow old with, climbing in the death zone suddenly seemed that little bit harder to convince myself to do.

I'd always said to myself that the moment my heart isn't in mountaineering, that is the moment I hang up my climbing boots. With the mountains, you need to accept that you might die pursuing your passion, so that passion better be so important and fulfilling that it is worth risking your life for. For me, that had been the case for many years, but now I'd grown up a little, and I started to feel my values changing and alarm bells starting to ring.

After everything I've learnt on Lhotse, have I lost my courage to climb up high again?

I asked myself this question many times when I considered never going back to K2. And it did feel like a question of courage. But courage comes in all guises – and perhaps the last thing that the mountains have taught me is that sometimes it can take just as much courage to step away from something, as it does to blindly carry on.

Over the years, I had come to fixate my identity on the mountains. Without them, I didn't know who I was. K2 was a chance to rekindle what I thought was my best self, but I hadn't realised that, after Lhotse, I had become so much more aware of how the simplest things in life can give us so much gratification, that you don't have to risk your life to truly live. I had now built a life challenging myself in so many other ways that didn't require facing my own mortality. I had come to realise that risking my life wasn't a necessary part of the equation when it came to taking huge and seemingly impossible challenges.

However, no matter what goals I set myself, if I was feeling low or lacking in confidence, telling myself that I could go and climb a mountain would always make me feel better. In some ways, the death zone had become my comfort zone – whenever I felt as if things weren't going well in life, I promised myself I'd get back to the mountains, and there I'd feel 'whole' again. The truth was, that kind of mentality was me just running from life, and hiding up in the hills. I wasn't that girl any more. I had to realise that, and I had to find passion in pushing myself in different ways.

When I was at the height of my mountaineering career, I'd always been a pretty shocking rock climber. I was an endurance athlete at my core, but my technical skills of balance and grip strength had been honed, just as my ability to stay on my feet for 24 hours at a time had. Mountains are generally climbed on two feet, while rock faces are climbed with fingertips and incredible core strength.

After K2, I made what I hoped was a courageous decision, not to go back to the big mountains again. Part of me felt bereft by this. I hadn't known when I stepped off Lhotse that it would be my last summit of an 8,000-metre peak. And now, facing a future without big Himalayan expeditions frightened me. But I knew that I needed to move forwards, and not keep returning to where I had become so comfortable, but so very close to tipping over the edge.

On that day, clinging to that cliff face above Railay Beach, I found myself talking to myself once more, reciting all the things I'd ever learnt from the mountains. *Just take a leap of faith. Trust yourself. You can do it. Don't be afraid to fall.*

Before I'd stepped on to the route, the hardest thing I'd ever tried to climb, Adrian kissed me on the forehead and said, 'Just remember to say to yourself, "I can and I will." Repeat it after me ...' and we both said together, 'I can and I will.'

Now, as my fingers tried to grip the sticky, sweaty ripple in the rock, I said to myself again: *I can and I will. I can and I will.* The last thing I can remember was being so focused on the handhold, my vision so tunnelled, that I forgot to be scared. *Focus on the detail. Focus on the process.* It was as though I was back, taking that first step on to the ladders in the Khumbu Icefall once again.

As I focused so intently, I found myself committing to the move. *What will be will be*, I thought, as I stepped my foot ever so delicately across, the rope dangling in mid-air between my legs. I felt a surge of adrenaline as the 'thank god jug' came within reach – wait for it! I stopped myself before I launched too soon, and made sure that my feet were secure before I finally lifted my left hand over my right and clasped my fingers around that huge jagged edge.

I exhaled with a massive sigh of relief. It felt as though everything I'd learnt in the mountains was still right there with me, pushing me on to do things I'd never thought I was capable of.

In life, we have to keep moving forwards, honing our skills and setting our sights on the things in life that are most meaningful to us. What you value now might be different in ten years' time, though. If anything, my experiences in the mountains had given me the wings I needed to take on the world in so many different ways, and as my values changed through life, I had all of those lessons with me in my heart.

Adrian cheered from below, 'You got this. Finish it.'

I looked up to the rest of the climb still towering above me, still the hardest section to do, and I thought to myself: *I can and I will.*

I can and I will.

ACKNOWLEDGEMENTS

This book wouldn't have been possible without the support of my partner, Adrian Baxter. From convincing me to write the initial proposal to offering his counsel when I was struggling the most, he believed in this project long before I did, and was there by my side throughout.

Thanks to Briony Gowlett from Hodder, to Jon Elek for representing me and also for introducing me to Kate Murray-Browne, who sat with me for many afternoons in Le Pain Quotidien whilst pregnant with baby Florence and wrote the first draft, helping me realise what the story was that I wanted to tell.

Thanks to my wonderful parents and family for your love and for being so resilient when I put you through many sleepless nights of angst and worry in pursuit of my dreams.

Thanks to those in the hills whose support and guidance is the reason this story exists to be told; Henry Todd, Rob Casserley, Kenton Cool and all those I've shared a rope or a tent with. Finally, thanks to Lhakpa Wongchu Sherpa and Rick Thurmer for not leaving me on the night of the 17th May 2010, and alongside the Himalayan Guides Sherpa team, undoubtedly saving my life.

BONITA NORRIS SUPPORTS PLAY FOR CHANGE

CHALLENGE YOURSELF to a sporting experience and raise money for Khelaun Khelaun, a Play for Change programme in Nepal that has already impacted 6,000 children and their communities through sport.

"WE CAN PUSH OURSELVES
FAR BEYOND WHAT WE
THINK WE ARE CAPABLE OF"
- BONITA NORRIS

Visit playforchange.org for more information

SHARE A PASSION. ENABLE CHANGE